North Meets South: Home Cooking

Jeanette Coniglio and Aimee Sheriff

Happy cooking!
Jeanette Coniglio

No Grits
No Glory
Enjoy!
Aimee Sheriff

PUBLISH AMERICA

PublishAmerica
Baltimore

First printing

ISBN: 1-4241-4799-9
PUBLISHED BY PUBLISHAMERICA, LLLP
www.publishamerica.com
Baltimore

Printed in the United States of America

Growing Up in the North

Being born and raised in the north (Long Island to be specific) I, Jeanette Coniglio, remember a childhood of hot and lazy summers, cool and colorful autumns, cold and snowy winters, and warm and flowery springs. Adulthood seemed light years away as childhood seemed to go on forever and ever. In those days, I just wanted to stay a child in the comfort and safety of my parents' home, surrounded by love, laughter, happiness and innocence. My family was and still is a tight-knit bunch. Of course, we had our sibling rivalries like most families; but all in all, our togetherness paved the way for some very wonderful and lasting memories that will be treasured forever in my heart.

Mealtime was a very important event in our family, because my parents insisted that we all eat together whenever possible. Saturday and Sunday mornings were probably the only two times during an entire week that all six family members were able to have breakfast together. Saturday was Mom's day to make breakfast for the family. We always had pancakes with lots of butter and maple syrup. I can still smell them cooking to this day. Sunday was Dad's turn. He loved to make bacon and eggs, and we ate them with Kaiser rolls and bagels that were purchased at a local bakery on the way home from church. My mouth still waters whenever I reminisce about the egg yolk oozing all over my plate, then soaking it up with a buttered roll. Most times lunches were impossible for all of us to enjoy together because of weekend activities and school during the week. Dinner was really the great family get-together every evening. Mom would have dinner ready just as Dad walked through the door from work. It would be a time when we all shared our happenings of the day with each other. Most of the time laughter reigned at the dinner table and left me with sweet memories today. Of course, the food was the main reason we gathered around the table in order to fill our bellies with the day's menu.

My mother, to this day, says that she never really "enjoyed" cooking, but she had to feed six people. I really think that deep down inside she just loved doing things for all of us, including planning and cooking the meals. One thing for sure is that she loved making a different dessert for us every night, from gingerbread, to pies and cakes, to puddings and Jell-O, and even brownies. Whenever I could, I would be in the kitchen watching my mother prepare dinners and/or desserts. I also remember thinking that I could not wait until I would be a grownup and be able to do the same for the family that I might someday have. Anyway, it was in that very kitchen where I grew up that I know for sure I developed the love for cooking, baking and concocting my own recipes.

My maternal grandmother was a wonderful cook and loved to bake, and I truly think I inherited her enthusiasm for being in the kitchen. Many Thanksgiving dinners were enjoyed at my grandparents' home during my childhood. It was a real treat to have dinner there. Her kitchen was small, but I tried to watch with great interest, and without getting in the way, at what she would do to create dinner and dessert. We always knew we were going to have a delectable culinary experience at Grandma's.

At the age of 37, I was already married for 15 years, and had two children. It was 1989; never wanting to shovel snow and shiver from the bitter cold anymore, my family moved to Florida, the Sunshine State, to begin a "new life." Unfortunately, my marriage crumbled, but my love for cooking, baking and concocting recipes did not.

I actually do have a "new life" now. I am happily married to my second husband, my children are two awesome adults, and I have three really terrific step-children. This book is dedicated to my husband, John, my "five" children, Andrea, Daniel, Theresa, John and Emily, and my mother, Jackie, who all fill my life and heart with the love, laughter, happiness, and innocence of my childhood, and to my father, Philip, and grandmother, Ethel, who although they have passed on, left me with many wonderful and loving memories.

Growing Up in the South

My goodness, where do I begin? Being raised in the South, I, Aimee Sheriff, am a fourth generation Floridian on my maternal side and a second generation Floridian on my paternal side. My father's family moved to Florida about 80 years ago from Jessup, Georgia, where they had once been farmers. So you can see my roots are very deep seeded in the South. My parents separated when I was six years old, and even though I lived between two homes, there was always something they shared in common...the love and welfare of their children and a passion for cooking.

I'll begin with my father, since one of my first memories of food began with him. I was about three or four when we traveled to Jessup, Georgia, for a family reunion. There had to have been about one hundred people at the reunion, or so it seemed to a young child. While the men were off roasting the pigs and barbequing the chickens they had slaughtered earlier, the women were setting up the banquet tables. I remember rows and rows of tables with mismatched tablecloths that were brought from each family's home. The tables were covered in all of these wonderful southern dishes from fresh garden vegetables to homemade casseroles, potato salad, slaws and desserts. I sat and watched these women talk, taste, and trade recipes, and I knew that this was a Southern ritual into which I had been born.

Weekends and vacations were spent with my Dad, and from a very young age we would discuss the meals that would be prepared while we were there. My favorites were my father's fried chicken, marinated London broil, and barbequed delicacies. He made the most wonderful lemon and basil vinaigrette and sometimes made extra for me to take home to my mother. Dad and I do not share very many meals together anymore, because he has since moved to Mt. Dora, Florida, but the memories will last a lifetime.

My mother was a single mom who worked hard to provide a good life for her children. A lot of our meals during the week were very basic. My favorite weeknight meal was scrambled eggs, bacon, grits and toast. I think grits was one of my first solid foods, after baby cereal. Sunday meals were always the best, because my mother made the best chicken and dumplings you have ever put into your mouth. However, the recipe came from my paternal grandmother.

Almost all of our holidays were spent with my maternal grandparents. The meats would be slow-cooking in my grandmother's oven, from the roast turkey at Thanksgiving to the prime rib roast at Christmas, to my favorite honey-cured ham at Easter. Easter was my favorite holiday at Grandma and Grandpa's. I remember my grandmother's beautiful garden was in full glory at Easter. The hidden, dyed Easter eggs would be so hard to find among the pansies, snap dragons, and Gerbers. Once they were all found, they would be peeled by the grandchildren. Then Grandma would make her famous deviled eggs. Once I graduated from "head-dishwasher," I was allowed to help in preparing some of the wonderful Easter dishes.

I would like to thank my husband, Terry, and my daughter, Savannah, for being so patient with me during the many, many months it took me to write down these recipes. It was not easy to transfer a "recipe of the mind" onto paper with the correct measurements. You just cannot write "a little of this or a little of that." To my husband's family and our friends for being my guinea pigs..."I don't think they minded very much!"

I would like to dedicate this book to these great Southern men and women who are my family. I hope I honor their memories and recipes by carrying on these wonderful Southern traditions of the heart and soul; and to my Mom…"I love you."

Sections

BREAKFASTS

North

South

APPETIZERS

North

South

SALADS

North

South

SOUPS

North

South

BEEF

North

South

CHICKEN

North

South

PORK

North

South

VEAL

North

South

SEAFOOD

North

South

PASTA

North

South

VEGETABLES

North

South

POTATOES

North

South

CASEROLES

North

South

DESSERTS

North

South

BREAKFAST

Northern Recipes

Old-Fashioned French Toast

4 eggs beaten
1 cup milk
1 tbs. brown sugar
1 tsp. cinnamon
½ tsp. nutmeg
1 tsp. vanilla
8 slices French bread
Confectioners' sugar for topping
Butter
Maple Syrup

Heat an electric skillet or griddle to 350 degrees. Coat with non-stick spray. In a medium mixing bowl stir together beaten eggs and milk. Add brown sugar, cinnamon, nutmeg, and vanilla and stir until sugar is dissolved. Dip bread slices into egg mixture soaking well and carefully place in skillet. Cook on each side until golden brown. Remove to a serving plate and sprinkle with confectioners' sugar. Serve with butter and warm maple syrup.

Old-Fashioned Buttermilk Pancakes

1 cup cake flour
1 ½ tsp. baking powder
½ tsp. baking soda
½ tsp. salt
2 tbs. sugar
1 egg
1 cup buttermilk
2 tbs. melted butter

In a medium mixing bowl, sift flour with baking powder, baking soda, salt, and sugar. Whisk in egg, buttermilk and butter until just combined. Batter will be lumpy. Heat griddle or electric frying pan to 375 degrees. Coat griddle with cooking spray. Using about ¼ cup batter for each pancake, drop batter onto griddle. Cook until bubbles form on top and sides of pancakes are a little dry. Flip over and cook until pancakes are golden brown. Serve pancakes with butter and warm maple syrup. You may add fresh blueberries to the batter before cooking for an old-fashioned taste.

Apple-Raisin Oat Bran Muffins

1/3 cup honey
½ cup oil
1 tsp. vanilla
2 eggs
1 ½ cups flour
1 cup oat bran
2 tsp. baking powder
1 tsp. baking soda
¼ tsp. salt
1 cup low-fat vanilla yogurt
1 cup applesauce
½ cup raisins
½ cup walnuts (optional)

In a large bowl, mix honey and oil. Whisk in vanilla and eggs. In a separate bowl, sift together flour, oat bran, baking powder, baking soda, and salt. Stir dry ingredients into wet. Add yogurt. Fold in applesauce, raisins and nuts. Place cupcake papers into muffin tins. Fill muffin cups to 2/3 full. Bake at 375 degrees for 20–25 minutes or until toothpick inserted into center of muffin comes out clean. Cool for 20 minutes, remove muffins from tins and continue to cool on rack.

Hungry Man Skillet Breakfast

6 strips bacon
½ of 1-lb. roll of sausage meat, broken up
2 potatoes, peeled and cut in small cubes
1 small green bell pepper, cut into small pieces
1 small red bell pepper, cut into small pieces
1 small onion, chopped
1 tsp. seasoned salt
Pepper
6 eggs, beaten with ¼ cup milk
½ cup shredded cheddar or Monterey Jack cheese

In a large skillet, cook bacon until crisp. Remove from skillet. Crumble. Set aside. Pour off bacon fat. In same skillet, cook sausage until well done. Remove from skillet. Set aside. Pour off all but 2 tbs. fat. Over medium heat sauté potatoes, peppers and onions until potatoes are cooked through. Sprinkle with seasoned salt and pepper to taste. Return bacon bits and sausage to skillet. Pour in egg mixture and stir until eggs are cooked. Top with shredded cheese. Serve immediately.

Scones

2 cups flour
1 tbs. baking powder
¼ cup butter (1/2 stick), softened
3 tbs. sugar
2 eggs
2 tbs. water
½ cup, plus 1 tbs. buttermilk
½ cup raisins (optional)

Sift flour and baking powder together. Set aside. In a separate bowl, beat butter and sugar together until light and fluffy. Beat 1 egg and add to the butter mixture. Add ½ cup buttermilk and blend well. Add flour mixture and mix with a fork or pastry blender until mixture resembles coarse crumbs. Add remaining buttermilk and mix until smooth. Stir in raisins. On lightly floured surface, roll out dough to ½ inch thick. Using 2 inch round cookie cutter, cut out scones and place on non-stick baking sheet or baking stone. Beat the remaining egg with water. Brush tops of scones with egg wash. Bake at 450 degrees for 15 minutes until risen and lightly browned. Makes about 15–18 scones.

Grandma's Buttermilk Biscuits

2 cups flour
2 ½ tsp. baking powder
½ tsp. baking soda
1/8 tsp. salt
2 tbs. sugar
½ cup shortening
¾ cup buttermilk

In large bowl, sift together flour, baking powder, baking soda, salt and sugar. Cut in shortening with pastry blender until mixture resembles coarse crumbs. Make a well in center and slowly add buttermilk, mixing quickly until just combined. Turn out onto lightly floured surface. Knead only two or three times, making soft dough. (Do not over knead or biscuits will not be soft.) Form dough into a 6 inch x 6 inch square. Divide dough into 12 equal parts by making slits (4 one way, 3 the other way) on top of dough, but DO NOT cut completely through. Place dough on ungreased baking sheet or baking stone. Dust dough with flour. Bake at 400 degrees for 15–20 minutes or until golden. Serve warm with butter and jam.

Southern Recipes

Bacon, Sausage, Egg, and Cheese Breakfast Quiche

1 package pie crust mix or ½ pie crust recipe from Apple Pie recipe in dessert section
6 large eggs
1 cup half and half
3 bacon strips cooked crisp and crumbled
3 breakfast sausage links cooked and diced
1 cup shredded cheddar cheese

Prepare pie crust mix according to package directions for a one-crust pie, or follow directions for homemade pie crust. Line pie pan with rolled out crust, trim, and flute edges. In a large mixing bowl, beat eggs well. Slowly whisk in half and half. Stir in bacon, sausage and shredded cheese. Pour mixture into prepared pie crust. Place pie pan on a large cookie sheet. Bake at 350 degrees for approximately 30 minutes or until mixture is set and toothpick inserted in middle comes out clean. Let cool for 10 minutes before serving.

Blueberry Sour Cream Pancakes

1 cup all-purpose flour
1 tsp. baking soda
2 tsp. baking powder
½ tsp. salt
2 tbs. sugar
1 egg
2 tbs. butter, melted
1 cup half and half
½ cup sour cream
1 cup of fresh or frozen blueberries (that have been thawed)

In a medium mixing bowl combine all ingredients except blueberries. Mix with wooden spoon until well blended. Gently fold in blueberries. Heat a frying pan or griddle to 350 degrees. Coat pan with non-stick cooking spray. Pour ¼ cup batter on griddle for each pancake. Cook until bubbles form on top, then flip over and continue cooking until pancakes are golden brown. Serve with butter and warm maple syrup or with whipped cream on top and additional fresh blueberries.

Biscuits and Sausage Gravy

1 can of biscuits
1 1-lb. roll of sausage meat, broken into small pieces
3 tbs. flour
2 ½ cups milk
5–8 dashes of Tabasco sauce (depending how "hot" you like it)
Salt and pepper

Bake biscuits according to package directions. Set aside. Meanwhile, heat a large skillet over medium heat and brown sausage meat until all pink is gone. Drain, reserving about 2 tbs. grease. Whisk in flour and continue stirring until a smooth paste forms. Slowly pour in milk while continuing to stir with whisk. Keep stirring until sauce is smooth and thickened. Add Tabasco sauce. Salt and pepper to taste. If sauce is too thick, stir in milk a little at a time until desired consistency is reached. Cut open a biscuit and place both halves on a plate. Spoon sausage gravy over biscuits. Continue this for each biscuit. Serve immediately.

This is also good with one or two fried eggs placed on top of gravy.

Grits

4 cups water
½ stick butter
1 cup quick cooking grits
1 ½ cups shredded cheddar cheese

Place water in a medium saucepan. Bring water to a boil. Add butter and grits. Reduce heat to low. Simmer for 15 minutes. Add shredded cheese. Continue simmering until all liquid is absorbed. Place grits in serving bowls. You can serve this with pat of butter on top.

APPETIZERS

Northern Recipes

Italian Sausage Bread

1 lb. pizza dough at room temperature
2 lbs. Italian sausage, squeezed from casings
½ lb. mozzarella cheese, shredded
1 small onion, chopped
2 cloves garlic, chopped
¾ cup each red and green bell pepper, chopped
¼ cup olive oil

Roll dough on lightly floured surface into a rectangular shape approximately 12" x 15". Spread raw sausage meat on dough leaving an inch border all around. Sprinkle mozzarella cheese over sausage. Place chopped onion, garlic and peppers evenly over cheese. Roll up dough lengthwise, jellyroll style, carefully folding in sides to seal. Place roll on non-stick baking sheet seam side down. Make slits across top of dough to vent. Brush with olive oil. Bake at 375 degrees for 45 minutes or until dough is golden brown. Cool slightly before slicing. Serve warm.

Jeanette's Stuffed Mushrooms

24 large mushrooms
Kosher salt
2 tbs. butter or margarine
4 tbs. olive oil
1 ½ cups Italian flavored bread crumbs
1/3 cup grated Romano or Parmesan cheese
3 cloves garlic, finely chopped
1 cup chopped scallions
1 small green bell pepper, finely chopped
½ cup cooked shrimp, chopped
½ cup cooked lump crab meat, chopped
1 cup finely shredded Monterey Jack cheese

Cut stems from mushrooms and chop into bits. Set aside. Lightly sprinkle mushroom caps with salt. In a large skillet, melt butter. Sauté mushroom caps on hollow side only. Remove from skillet. Set aside. In a medium bowl, combine mushroom stem bits with bread crumbs and grated cheese. Set aside. In a small skillet, heat oil over low-medium heat and sauté garlic, scallions, and green pepper. Add bread crumb mixture (add more bread crumbs if mixture is too wet.) Add shrimp and crabmeat and mix until well incorporated. Place a generous teaspoonful of mixture into each mushroom cap. Arrange mushrooms in a baking pan. Bake at 375 degrees for 20 minutes or until bread crumb mixture browns. Remove from oven. Sprinkle with shredded cheese. Return to oven and bake for an additional 5–10 minutes or until cheese is melted.

Swedish Meatballs

1 ½ lbs. ground beef
¾ lb. ground pork
3 eggs
½ cup finely chopped onion
1 cup half & half
Salt and pepper
½ tsp. allspice
1 cup plain bread crumbs

Sauce

3 tbs. flour
¾ cup half & half
Salt and pepper
1 15-oz. can beef broth
¼ tsp. allspice

In a large bowl combine beef and pork, eggs, onion, half & half, salt and pepper to taste, allspice and bread crumbs. Mix until well blended. Shape into small meatballs. In large frying pan, melt butter over low-medium heat and sauté meatballs until browned on all sides. Remove meatballs. In 2 tbs. drippings, stir in flour. Gradually add half & half and beef broth. Bring to a boil, stirring constantly to avoid lumps from forming. Add salt, pepper to taste and allspice. Add the meatballs and stir. Heat through. Garnish with parsley flakes.

This recipe can also be used as an entrée by making the meatballs larger and serving them over wide noodles.

Deep Dish Italian Pie

1 medium onion, chopped
½ lb. sliced mushrooms
2–3 tbs. olive oil
1 lb. pizza dough at room temperature
1 tbs. heavy cream
1 egg yolk
½ lb. ham cappicolla, thinly sliced
½ lb. Genoa salami, thinly sliced
½ lb. pepperoni, thinly sliced
½ lb. Sliced provolone cheese
2 7-oz. jars roasted red bell peppers, drained and cut into thin strips
2 14-oz. cans artichoke hearts, drained and coarsely chopped
1 6-oz. can small pitted ripe olives, drained and halved
½ lb. part-skim mozzarella cheese, shredded

In a large frying pan, sauté onion and mushrooms in olive oil over medium heat, just until soft, do not brown. Drain to remove excess oil. Transfer to a bowl and set aside. On a floured surface, roll 2/3 dough into a 15–16 inch circle. Press dough evenly into a lightly greased 10" spring form pan covering bottom and sides. In a small bowl, beat heavy cream with egg yolk until well blended. Brush lightly over dough, reserving excess for glaze. Fill dough-lined pan in layers as follows: ham, salami, pepperoni, and provolone cheese, 1/3 of the mushroom and onion mixture, 1/3 of the pepper strips, 1/3 of the artichoke hearts, 1/3 of the olives, and 1/3 of the shredded mozzarella cheese. Repeat 2 more times. Roll out remaining third of dough into a 10" circle, brush with remaining glaze. Place dough glazed-side down over filling. Press edges together to seal, tucking them under. Make slits in top dough to vent. Brush top with any remaining glaze. Bake at 375 degrees for 35–45 minutes or until pie is heated through the inside and golden on the outside. Loosen pie from sides of pan with a knife and remove outer part of pan. Let it cool uncovered for up to 2 hours. Cut into wedges and serve warm.

Southern Recipes

Ham and Cheddar Roll with Honey Mustard Sauce

1 lb. pizza dough
½ lb. sliced deli ham
2 cups shredded cheddar cheese
2 tbs. melted butter

Lightly flour a smooth surface. Roll out pizza dough to about a 12" x 16" rectangle. Place ham slices over dough leaving about an inch around edge of dough. Top with the cheddar cheese. Starting on long edge, roll up jelly-roll style folding in the ends as you roll. Place on a baking sheet or a pizza stone seam-side down. Using a sharp knife, make slits on top to vent. Bake at 400 degrees for 30 minutes. Brush with melted butter and continue baking for 5–10 minutes more. Let cool for 20 minutes, and then cut into slices.

Honey Mustard Sauce

2 tbs. yellow or Dijon mustard
1 tbs. honey
1 cup mayonnaise

Combine all ingredients in a small mixing bowl until well blended. Transfer to serving bowl. Dip slices of ham roll into sauce and enjoy.

Grandma's Deviled Eggs

1 dozen large eggs
½ cup mayonnaise
3 tbs. yellow mustard
2 tbs. relish juice
1 tsp. salt
Paprika
Chopped black olives (optional)

Place eggs in a large pot, cover with water and boil for 10–12 minutes. Drain hot water from pot and let cold water run over eggs for about 1 minute. Remove eggs from pot, place eggs on paper towels, and let cool completely. Peel eggs and cut in half lengthwise. Place egg yolks in a medium mixing bowl and place all empty egg whites on a serving platter. In a small mixing bowl, combine mayonnaise, mustard, relish juice, and salt and mix until well blended. You may also put these ingredients in a blender and mix until well blended. Place a heaping teaspoonful of yolk mixture into the egg whites. Sprinkle with a little paprika and top with chopped olives. Chill before serving.

Aimee's Stuffed Mushrooms

1 lb. hot Italian sausage, squeezed out of casings
1 container of large stuffing mushrooms (approximately 10–12 mushrooms)
1 cup shredded sharp cheddar cheese

Preheat a large skillet over low-medium heat and sauté sausage meat until all pink is gone. Drain to remove grease. In a medium mixing bowl, combine sausage meat and cheddar cheese. Set aside. Remove stems from mushrooms and scrape dark filament from inside mushrooms caps. Fill caps with sausage mixture. Bake at 350 degrees for about 30–40 minutes until cheese is melted and slightly browned on top. You can also choose to microwave on high until completely cooked through and cheese melted on top.

Guacamole

2–3 very ripe avocados
1 small onion, finely chopped
1 plum tomato, finely chopped
2 tbs. fajita seasoning (from a packet)
Juice of 1 lemon
¼ cup sour cream

Peel avocados and remove fruit from the pit. Place in a medium mixing bowl. Mash well using a potato masher. Add rest of ingredients and continue mashing until mixture becomes creamy, but still has some small pieces. Place into a serving bowl and chill for several hours. Serve with tortilla chips for dipping.

SALADS

Northern Recipes

Italian Pasta Salad

½ lb. bowtie pasta, cooked and cooled, set aside
½ lb. cheese tortellini, cooked and cooled, set aside
1/3 cup balsamic vinegar
2 tsp. water
1 cup olive oil
2 garlic cloves, crushed
½ tsp. dried basil
½ tsp. dried oregano
¼ tsp. dried marjoram
¼ tsp. dried summer savory
¼ tsp. dried parsley flakes
½ tsp. salt
¼ tsp. pepper
1 lb. broccoli flowerets, lightly steamed and cooled
½ lb. carrots, julienne
½ lb. grape tomatoes cut in half
1 15-oz. can small black olives, drained
2 4-oz. jars whole mushrooms, drained
1 15-oz. can artichoke hearts, drained, cut into quarters
1 each red, yellow, green bell pepper, cut into small pieces

In a medium bowl, mix together the vinegar, water, olive oil, garlic, basil, oregano, marjoram, savory, parsley flakes, salt and pepper, until well blended. In large salad bowl, place bowtie pasta, tortellini, broccoli florets, julienne carrots, grape tomatoes, olives, mushrooms, artichoke hearts, and peppers. Toss until well combined. Pour vinaigrette mixture over pasta and toss until pasta and vegetables are well coated. Refrigerate for several hours and toss again before serving.

Fresh Green Bean Salad

1 ½ lb. fresh green beans, trimmed, washed and drained
2 ripe medium-size tomatoes cut in wedges
2 15-oz. cans quartered artichoke hearts, drained
1 small red onion sliced very thin
½ lb. fresh white mushroom slices, rinsed and drained
1 cup olive oil
1/3 cup red wine vinegar
2 tsp. water
Salt and pepper to taste
2 cloves garlic, crushed
½ tsp. dried parsley flakes
½ tsp. dried oregano
½ tsp. dried basil
¼ tsp. sugar

Place green beans in a large pot, cover with water and bring to a boil. Reduce heat and simmer, covered for about 4 minutes or until green beans turn very green. Remove from heat and drain. Rinse with cold water immediately until completely cooled. Place in a large salad bowl. Add tomato wedges, artichoke hearts, onion slices and mushrooms. Toss lightly. In a separate small bowl, blend together all remaining ingredients. Pour over green bean mixture and toss until all vegetables are well coated. Cover and refrigerate for several hours. Toss again before serving.

Sunshine Salad

½ cup canola oil
1/3 cup frozen orange juice concentrate
1/3 cup honey
2 tbs. apple cider vinegar
1 ½ tsp. salt
1 ½ tsp. sugar
1 tsp. dry mustard
1 tsp. paprika
Dash pepper
4 cups torn salad greens
2 tomatoes sliced in wedges
1 cup snow peas
1 small red pepper cut into thin slices
1 small red onion cut into thin rings
1 11-oz. can mandarin oranges, drained
¾ cup chopped walnuts, toasted

In a small mixing bowl, blend together the oil, orange juice concentrate, honey, vinegar, salt, sugar, dry mustard, paprika, and pepper to make salad dressing. Chill for several hours. In a large salad bowl, toss together salad greens, tomato wedges, snow peas, red pepper slices, and onion rings. Toss in oranges. Add walnuts and toss until well blended. Chill. Just before serving, pour dressing over salad mixture and toss until well blended. Serve immediately to prevent greens from wilting.

Tomato Basil Salad

4 large ripe tomatoes cut into wedges
1 red onion, very thinly sliced
10 fresh basil leaves, chopped
½ cup fresh Italian parsley, chopped
1 lb. fresh mozzarella cheese cut in small chunks
¼ cup red wine vinegar
¾ cup olive oil
2 garlic cloves, minced
Salt and pepper
½ tsp. dried marjoram
4 scallions sliced into ¼ inch rings

In a large salad bowl, combine tomato wedges, onion slices, basil leaves and parsley. Chill for several hours. Add mozzarella cheese. In a small mixing bowl, blend together the vinegar, olive oil, minced garlic. Add salt and pepper to taste and the marjoram. Stir until well combined. Chill several hours. About 30 minutes before serving, pour dressing over the tomato mixture and toss to coat well and allow flavors to blend together. Top with sliced scallions.

Southern Recipes

Cole Slaw

1 1-lb bag shredded cabbage
2 tbs. white vinegar
¼ cup, minus 2 tbs. sugar
¾ cup mayonnaise
2 tbs. dried parsley

Place shredded cabbage in a large mixing bowl. In a small mixing bowl, combine vinegar, sugar, mayonnaise, and dried parsley and mix until well blended. Pour mixture over cabbage and toss until well coated. Chill for several hours, tossing occasionally.

Potato Salad

5 lbs. red-skinned potatoes
½ red onion, diced
2 celery ribs, finely chopped
4 hard boiled eggs, chopped
2 cups mayonnaise
¼ cup mustard
2 tbs. pickle juice
Salt and pepper

Place whole potatoes in a large pot and cover completely with water. Bring potatoes to a boil and cook until potatoes are fork tender (do not over boil). Transfer potatoes to a platter and let cool. (You may cool them in the refrigerator if you wish). Cut potatoes into chunks and place into a large mixing bowl. Add onion, celery, and eggs. Using a wooden spoon, gently toss potato mixture. Add mayonnaise, mustard, pickle juice and salt and pepper to taste. Gently mix until well blended. Chill for several hours before serving.

Black Bean Salad

1 15-oz. can black beans, drained and rinsed
1 15-oz. can diced tomatoes with green chilies
1 11-oz. can white corn, drained
1 small red onion, peeled and diced
1 small packet of dry ranch dressing mix

In a medium bowl, combine all ingredients. Transfer to a serving bowl, cover and refrigerate for several hours before serving.

This is also great served warm. Just heat before serving.

Avocado Salad

2 ripe avocados, peeled and diced
1 large tomato, chopped
1 small red onion, peeled and finely chopped
Juice of 1 lemon
2 tbs. olive oil
Salt and pepper

In a large mixing bowl, combine diced avocados, chopped tomato, and red onion. Add the lemon juice, olive oil, and salt and pepper to taste. Transfer to serving bowl. Refrigerate for several hours before serving.

SOUPS

Northern Recipes

New England Clam Chowder

6 strips bacon
2 tbs. butter
2 ribs of celery cut into pieces
2 medium potatoes, peeled and cut into cubes
2 bottles clam juice
3 cups half and half or whole milk
Salt and pepper
1 tsp. fresh parsley, chopped
2 cans chopped clams with juice

In non-stick frying pan, fry bacon until crisp, drain, cool, crumble, set aside. In 4-quart soup pot melt butter over medium heat. Sauté celery and potatoes for 5 minutes. Add clam juice and bring to a light boil. Reduce heat and simmer for 10 minutes, or until potatoes are almost cooked. Slowly add half and half, salt and pepper, and parsley. Bring to light boil. Reduce heat and simmer for 10 minutes more. Stir in chopped clams and crumbled bacon, and heat through. Serve in soup bowls with oyster crackers.

Tomato Tortellini Soup

2 tbs. butter
2 medium onions, coarsely chopped
2 ribs of celery cut in slices crosswise
2 14-oz. cans chicken broth
2 14-oz. cans whole peeled tomatoes, chopped, reserve liquid
1 6-oz. can tomato paste
½ tsp. salt
¼ tsp. black pepper
1 tsp. summer savory
½ tsp. dried parsley flakes
1 9-oz. bag frozen tortellini with cheese
Grated Parmesan and Romano cheese

In 4-quart soup pot, melt butter over low heat and sauté onions and celery until onions become transparent, do not brown. Add chicken broth, tomatoes with reserved liquid, and tomato paste. Stir until well blended. Sprinkle with salt and pepper. Add summer savory and parsley flakes. Bring to light boil, reduce heat and simmer for 45 minutes. Meanwhile, in separate pot, cook tortellini according to package directions. Drain. Spoon tortellini into soup bowls and ladle tomato soup over tortellini. Sprinkle with grated cheese.

Minestrone with Mini-Meatballs

2 tbs. butter
2 medium onions, peeled and coarsely chopped
2 cloves garlic, chopped
3 carrots, peeled, and cut into slices
3 stalks celery, cut into slices crosswise
5 14-oz. cans low-salt beef broth
½ lb. fresh green beans cut into 1 inch pieces
½ lb. fresh mushrooms, sliced
1 medium zucchini cut in half lengthwise, then into slices
Salt and pepper
Mini-Meatballs, recipe follows
1 15-oz. can navy beans, drained
8 oz. orzo or acini de pepe pasta cooked according to package directions

In large soup pot, melt butter over low heat and sauté onions, garlic, carrots, and celery until onion becomes transparent, do not brown. Add beef broth. Bring to light boil, reduce heat and simmer 5 minutes. Add green beans, mushrooms, zucchini, salt and pepper to taste, and meatballs. Simmer 15 minutes. Add navy beans. Heat through. Ladle soup over orzo pasta in large soup bowls.

Mini-Meatballs

1 lb. ground beef
½ lb. ground pork
2 eggs
Dash salt and black pepper

½ tsp. garlic powder
½ tsp. dried basil
½ tsp. dried oregano
¼ tsp. dried parsley flakes
½ cup Italian flavored bread crumbs
Milk to soak bread crumbs

In medium mixing bowl, blend ground beef and ground pork, eggs, salt, pepper, garlic powder, basil, oregano and parsley flakes, until mixture is smooth. In separate small mixing bowl, blend bread crumbs with enough milk to soak bread crumbs. Add bread crumb mixture to meat mixture and mix until well blended. With palms of hands, form meat mixture into small meatballs. Place in shallow baking pan, bake in oven at 375 for 30 minutes.

Pasta e Fagioli (Pasta Fazool)

2 tbs. olive oil
5 cloves garlic, peeled and chopped
1 carrot, peeled and cut into small pieces
1 rib celery cut into small pieces
2 28-oz. can tomatoes, chopped, reserve liquid
2 tbs. fresh basil, chopped
1 tbs. marjoram
Salt and pepper
½ tsp. sugar
2 19-oz. cans cannellini beans
8 oz. Ditilini pasta (or any small pasta)

In 4 qt. soup pot, heat olive oil over low-medium heat. Sauté garlic, carrots and celery for 2–3 minutes; do not brown garlic. Add tomatoes with reserved liquid, basil and marjoram, salt and pepper to taste, and sugar. Bring to light boil, reduce heat and simmer 30 minutes. Meanwhile in separate pot, cook ditilini pasta according to package directions. Drain. Set aside. Gently stir cannellini beans into soup mixture. Heat through. Spoon pasta into soup bowls. Ladle soup over pasta. Sprinkle with grated Romano cheese.

Southern Recipes

Chicken Noodle Soup

2 tbs. olive oil
1 small onion, chopped
3 carrots, peeled and chopped
2 cloves garlic, finely chopped
4 cups chicken broth
2 cups water
1 ½ lbs. boneless, skinless chicken thighs
2 tsp. Italian seasonings
Salt and pepper to taste
1 tbs. dried parsley
1 tbs. garlic salt
2 cups extra wide egg noodles

Heat olive oil over medium heat in a large soup pot. Sauté onion, carrots, and garlic until onion becomes transparent. Add chicken broth and water. Bring to a boil. Add chicken thighs; reduce heat, cover, and simmer until thighs are cooked. Transfer chicken thighs to a plate. Set aside to cool. Add all seasonings to broth and continue to simmer until chicken is cooled. Remove chicken from bones and chop into bite-size pieces. Return to broth. Bring to a boil again. Add egg noodles and continue to boil until noodles are al-dente. Serve hot.

Cajun Chicken and Sausage Stew

1 ½ lbs. boneless, skinless chicken breast cut into chunks
2 tbs. olive oil
1 ½ lbs. uncooked Kielbasa sausage cut into slices
1 cup chopped onion
½ cup chopped celery
½ cup chopped green bell pepper
½ cup chopped red bell pepper
1 clove garlic, chopped
2 tbs. Cajun seasoning
1 tbs. sugar
1 tsp. chili powder
2 14 ½-oz. cans zesty diced tomatoes with green chilies
Hot sauce

Heat olive oil in a large soup pot over medium heat. Sauté chicken until lightly browned, but not cooked through. Remove and set aside. Sauté Kielbasa until browned on all sides. Remove and set aside. Add onions, celery, green pepper, red pepper and garlic and sauté until onion becomes transparent. Stir in seasonings. Add canned tomatoes, chicken and Kielbasa. Simmer on low-medium heat for 20–30 minutes. Serve over white rice. For an extra kick, add a couple splashes of hot sauce.

Simple Seafood Chowder

2 boxes dry Leek Soup and Dip Recipe Mix
1 14 ½-oz. can diced new potatoes
2 cups frozen corn
1 6-oz. can fancy lump crab, partially drained
1 6 ½ oz. can chopped clams, partially drained
1 pt. heavy whipping cream
3 cups milk
1 tsp. Old Bay Seasoning
Salt and pepper
½ lb. shrimp, peeled and de-veined

In a large saucepot, combine all ingredients except the shrimp. Simmer over low heat for 30 minutes. Add shrimp. Continue to simmer until shrimp turn pink. Serve immediately.

Southern-Style Beef Stew

½ cup flour
1 tsp. seasoned salt
½ tsp. pepper
1 ½-2 lbs. top round beef cut into cubes
3 tbs. vegetable oil
1 14-oz. can low-salt beef broth
½ cup red wine
1 14 ½-oz. can diced tomatoes with liquid
¾ cup water
1 cup pearl onions
1 cup baby carrots
1 cup celery slices
1 cup frozen corn kernels
1 cup sliced fresh mushrooms
1 29-oz. can whole new potatoes
Salt and pepper

Place flour, seasoned salt, and pepper in a Ziploc bag. Add beef cubes a little at a time and shake well making sure beef is well coated. Place oil in a large soup pot and heat over medium heat. Add beef and brown. Drain. Return beef to pot. Add beef broth, red wine, diced tomatoes and water. Stir in pearl onions, carrots, and celery. Bring broth to a boil, reduce heat, cover and simmer for 45 minutes. Add corn, mushrooms, and potatoes. Salt and pepper to taste. Continue to simmer for approximately 30 minutes longer. Great served over wide noodles or rice.

BEEF

Northern Recipes

Old-Fashioned Pot Roast

3 tbs. canola oil
4–5 lb. rump roast (bottom round roast or beef brisket)
1 large onion, cut into thick vertical slices
4 cloves garlic, chopped
Salt and pepper
¼ tsp. marjoram
¼ tsp. summer savory
½ tsp. dried parsley
2 bay leaves
1 14 ½-oz. can low-salt beef broth
½ cup dry red wine
4 medium potatoes
4 carrots, peeled, cut into 1" pieces
2 tbs. flour
¾ cup water

In a large pot, heat oil over medium heat. Brown rump roast on all sides. When browning last side of meat, add onion slices, chopped garlic, salt and pepper to taste. When onions are soft and almost browned, add marjoram, summer savory, parsley, and bay leaves. Pour in broth and wine. Bring liquid to a boil, reduce heat, cover, and simmer for 2 ½ hours. Add potatoes and carrots and continue cooking for 30 minutes longer. Remove roast from pot. Remove bay leaves and discard. Transfer potatoes and carrots to a covered serving dish and keep warm.

In a shaker, mix flour and water. Shake until well blended. Slowly pour into gravy mixture, stirring constantly until gravy thickens and heats through. Slice roast. Serve with potatoes, carrots, and onion gravy.

Steak and Peppers

3 tbs. canola oil
2–3 lbs. top round steak, thinly sliced and cut into 1" strips
2 medium onions, thickly sliced
3 garlic cloves, chopped
Salt and pepper
½ tsp. ground ginger
¼ cup light soy sauce
1 14-oz. can low-salt beef broth
1 large green bell pepper, cut into strips
1 medium red bell pepper, cut into strips
2 tbs. flour
¾ cup water

In large pot, heat 3 tbs. oil over medium heat, brown steak strips until all pink is gone. Remove from pot. Discard drippings. In same pot, heat 2 tbs. oil, sauté onion and garlic until onion is transparent. Place meat back in pot, sprinkle with salt and pepper to taste, and add ginger. Stir in soy sauce and beef broth. Bring to a slow boil, reduce heat, and slowly simmer for 45 minutes. Add pepper strips and let simmer 20 min. longer. Meanwhile, mix flour with water and make a thick paste removing any lumps. Slowly, stir into beef mixture and constantly stir until gravy thickens. Remove from heat. Serve over rice or noodles.

Beef Stroganoff

3 tbs. canola oil, divided
1 ½ lb. flank steak, cut crosswise into ½ inch slices
1 medium onion, chopped
2 cloves garlic, chopped
½ lb. fresh whole mushrooms
3 tbs. flour
2 tbs. tomato paste
½ tsp. salt
1/8 tsp pepper
1 14-oz. can low-salt beef broth
¼ cup dry white wine
1 tsp. dried summer savory
1 cup sour cream
½ lb. extra wide noodles

Slowly heat 2 tbs. oil in a heavy skillet. Add just enough beef strips to cover bottom. Sear on both sides. Remove beef as it browns. Brown rest of beef and set aside. Discard drippings. Add remaining 1 tbs. oil. Sauté chopped onion, garlic and mushrooms until onion is golden. Remove from heat. Add flour, tomato paste, salt, pepper. Stir until mixture is smooth. Slowly add beef broth. Bring to boil, continuing to stir. Reduce heat. Simmer for 5 minutes. Add wine and summer savory. Return beef to pot. Heat through. Gently stir in sour cream until well blended. Meanwhile, boil noodles according to package directions, drain. Serve stroganoff over noodles.

Chili con Carne over Macaroni (Chili-Mac)

2 tbs. canola oil
1 medium onion, chopped
1 ½ lb. ground beef
1 15-oz. can tomatoes, chopped, reserve liquid
2 8-oz. cans tomato sauce
4 jalapeno peppers, de-seeded and cut into small pieces
2 packets chili seasoning
1 cup water
1 15-oz. can red kidney beans
8 oz. elbow macaroni
Shredded cheddar cheese
Sour cream (optional)

In a medium saucepan, heat 2 tbs. oil over low-medium heat. Sauté onion until transparent. Brown ground beef in same pan until all pink is gone. Drain in strainer to remove grease. Return onion and beef to saucepan. Add tomatoes, with liquid, tomato sauce, and jalapeno peppers. Sprinkle with seasonings. Add water. Mix until well blended. Simmer 30 minutes. Add beans. Simmer an additional 20 minutes. Meanwhile cook elbow macaroni according to package directions. Drain. Serve chili over elbow macaroni and sprinkle with shredded cheddar cheese. Add a dollop of sour cream on top.

Southern Recipes

Barbequed Beef Brisket

1 ½ cups of barbeque sauce, divided
1 small onion, chopped
1 4–5 lb. beef brisket

In a 5 or 6 quart crock pot, pour 1 cup barbeque sauce in bottom of pot. Add chopped onion. Gently place brisket on top and cover with remaining ½ cup barbeque sauce. Cover. Set temperature dial to low and cook for approximately 10 hours, or on high and cook for approximately 5 hours. Beef will be fork tender. Carefully remove brisket from crock pot keeping it from falling apart and place in a baking pan. Cover with aluminum foil and refrigerate overnight. (Chilling the brisket overnight keeps it from shredding apart when slicing.) Pour barbeque sauce with onions into a container and refrigerate until ready to use. The next day, heat grill on high. Reduce heat and cook brisket to warm through. Meanwhile, in a small saucepan, heat saved barbeque sauce with onions until lightly bubbly. Transfer brisket to carving board and slice. Place on serving platter and pour sauce over meat. Serves 10–12 people.

Aimee's Meatloaf

¾ lb. ground round
¾ lb. ground veal
¾ lb. ground pork
2 eggs
1 small onion, finely chopped
½ cup green bell pepper, finely chopped
1 packet of dry leek soup mix
1 tbs. Worcestershire sauce
2 tsp. hot sauce
½ cup ketchup, divided
¾ cup seasoned bread crumbs

In a large mixing bowl, blend together all of the ground meat. Mix in the eggs. Add onion, green pepper, soup mix, Worcestershire sauce, hot sauce and ¼ cup ketchup. Mix until well blended. Add the bread crumbs and mix again until well blended. Form meat mixture into a loaf shape and place in a roasting pan. Spread remaining ¼ cup ketchup on top. Cover pan with aluminum foil. Bake at 350 degrees for 45 minutes. Remove aluminum foil and continue baking for 20 minutes or until juices run clear and top is browned.

Beef Kabobs

1 ½ lbs. top round sirloin beef, cut into 1 inch cubes
1 zucchini, cut into ½ inch rings
½ large onion cut into quarters
1 8 oz. package of whole white mushrooms
1 cup pineapple chunks
1 cup pineapple juice
1 tbs. hoisin sauce
1 tbs. soy sauce
1 clove garlic, finely chopped

Place beef, zucchini, onion quarters, mushrooms and pineapple chunks into a large Ziploc bag. Meanwhile in a small mixing bowl, blend together the pineapple juice, hoisin sauce, soy sauce and chopped garlic. Pour mixture into Ziploc bag over meat and vegetables. Using 8-inch wooden skewers that have been soaked in water, place meat and vegetables alternating pieces on each skewer. Preheat grill on high. Place skewers on grill and cook until vegetables are tender.

Country Fried Steak

4 cubed steaks
½ tsp. salt
¼ tsp. pepper
1 cup flour, plus 3 tbs.
½ cup crushed saltine crackers
1 tsp. black pepper
1 egg
½ cup milk, plus 3 cups
Salt and pepper
1 cup vegetable oil

Season steaks with salt and pepper to taste. In a small mixing bowl, mix 1 cup flour with crushed crackers and 1 tsp. pepper. In a separate bowl, beat egg with ½ cup milk. Dredge each steak in flour mixture, through egg wash, and back through flour mixture again. Shake off excess flour. In a large skillet or electric frying pan, heat oil to 350 degrees. Fry steaks until golden brown on both sides. Drain on paper towels, place on platter and set aside. Pour out all but ¼ cup oil from skillet. Whisk in the remaining 3 tbs. flour and stir until smooth. Add the remaining 3 cups milk, salt and pepper to taste, stirring constantly until mixture thickens. Pour gravy over steak and serve with your favorite sides.

CHICKEN

Northern Recipes

Chicken Cordon Bleu

8 boneless chicken breasts, butterflied and flattened
8 slices deli ham
8 slices baby Swiss cheese
2 cups flour
4 eggs, beaten, mixed with ½ cup milk
3 cups flavored breadcrumbs
1 cup canola oil
¼ cup butter or margarine (1/2 stick)
¼ cup flour
1 cup milk
1 cup low-salt chicken broth
Dash pepper

Place chicken breasts on flat surface. Place a slice of ham and a slice of Swiss cheese on each breast. Roll each breast and secure with several toothpicks. Roll chicken breasts in flour, dip into egg mixture, then cover completely with breadcrumbs, especially on the ends to secure the cheese. Meanwhile, heat oil in large frying pan. Brown each chicken roll on all sides, remove from heat and drain on paper towels.

Place chicken rolls in baking dish and bake at 350 degrees for 30–40 minutes.

Meanwhile, during last 10 minutes of baking time, melt butter in skillet. Whisk in flour to make a roux making sure there are no lumps.

Slowly add milk and chicken broth, stirring constantly until mixture is smooth and thickens. Sprinkle with pepper.

Transfer chicken to serving platter. Pour sauce over chicken and serve with rice, fluffy mashed potatoes (see Potato section for recipe), or medium noodles.

Chicken (or Beef) Ragout over Noodles

6 slices of bacon
3 tbs. canola oil
2 ½ lbs. boneless chicken breasts cut into 1 inch pieces
Salt & pepper
1 14-oz. can beef broth
1 ¼ cups water, divided
½ cup dry white wine
2 cloves garlic, crushed
1 large bay leaf
1 jar pearl onions
2 15-oz. cans slices carrots
1 15-oz. can sliced mushrooms
2 tbs. flour
½ lb. extra wide noodles

In a large skillet, fry bacon. Drain and crumble. Set aside. In large saucepan, heat oil. Brown chicken lightly on all sides. Sprinkle with salt and pepper to taste. Add broth, 1 cup water, wine, garlic, and bay leaf. Cover, simmer 20 min. Remove bay leaf and discard. Pour in vegetables, simmer 20 min. In a shaker combine flour with remaining ¼ cup water and shake until mixture is smooth. Slowly pour flour mixture into broth stirring constantly until well blended. Stir in crumbled bacon. Meanwhile, cook noodles according to package directions. Serve chicken ragout over noodles. May also be served over rice.

Note: Beef cut in cubes may be substituted for chicken…change chicken broth to beef broth, and dry white wine to dry red wine.

Balsamic Chicken Portabella and Mozzarella Grill

¼ cup balsamic vinegar
¾ cup olive oil
¼ tsp. garlic powder
¼ tsp. salt
1/8 tsp. ground black pepper
¼ tsp. dried marjoram
¼ tsp. dried basil
½ tsp. dried parsley flakes
6 boneless, skinless chicken breasts
2 tbs. olive oil
12 slices portabella mushrooms
½ lb. part-skim mozzarella cheese, thinly sliced

In a small bowl, mix together first 8 ingredients to make balsamic vinaigrette. Place chicken breasts in a shallow baking dish. Pour balsamic vinaigrette over chicken, coating all pieces. Cover and place in refrigerator for several hours to marinate.

Heat barbeque grill on high for 10 minutes. Meanwhile, in a large skillet, heat oil over medium heat. Sauté mushroom slices until softened. Remove from skillet and drain. Set aside. Reduce heat on grill to low. Grill chicken breasts until cooked through, but not dry. Place 2 mushroom slices on each chicken breast and 2 slices of cheese over the mushrooms. Cover grill and continue cooking until cheese is melted. Remove from grill and serve.

Chicken Cacciatore

1 3–4 lb. chicken, cut up
½ cup flour
¼ cup canola oil
1 large onion, thinly sliced into rings
1 medium green pepper, cut into strips
1 cup sliced fresh mushrooms
3 cloves garlic, chopped
1 14 ½-oz. can tomatoes, roughly chopped, reserve liquid
1 15-oz. can tomato sauce
¼ cup dry red wine
Salt and pepper
½ tsp. dried oregano
½ tsp. dried basil
½ tsp. sugar

Coat chicken with flour. In a large skillet, heat oil over medium heat. Brown chicken on all sides, about 20 minutes. Remove chicken. Set aside. In same skillet, add onion rings, pepper strips, mushrooms, and garlic. Sauté until onions are soft. Add tomatoes with liquid, tomato sauce, and wine. Salt and pepper to taste. Add oregano, basil and sugar and stir to blend well. Return chicken to skillet. Reduce heat, cover and simmer for 45 minutes or until chicken is cooked through, stirring sauce every 10 minutes to prevent sticking to bottom of skillet. Serve over rice or noodles.

Southern Recipes

Terry's Favorite Southern Fried Chicken

1 whole fryer chicken cut up
1 cup milk
2 eggs
3 cups flour
1/3 cup seasoned salt
1 tbs. black pepper
1 tsp. baking powder
Peanut oil

In a small bowl, mix milk and eggs together. Set aside. In a medium bowl, mix together the flour, seasoned salt, pepper, and baking powder until well blended. Pour dry mixture into a Ziploc bag. Dip chicken pieces one at a time into milk, egg mixture. Dredge chicken into flour mixture in Ziploc bag and shake well. Place pieces of chicken on a platter and refrigerate for about an hour. Place about an inch or inch and a half of oil into a large frying pan. Heat oil to about 350 degrees. Dredge chicken a second time into flour mixture. Gently place chicken into heated oil and cook for approximately 6–8 minutes on each side. Dark meat may take a little longer. Place several sheets of paper towels in the bottom of a brown paper bag. Drain chicken in bag for a few minutes leaving top of bag open. Transfer to serving platter and serve immediately.

Chicken and Dumplings Southern Style

1 3–4 lb. fryer chicken
½ onion
Salt and pepper
1 ½ cups flour
5 tbs. shortening
3 tbs. cold milk

Place chicken in a large pot and cover with water. Add the ½ onion. Bring to a boil. Reduce heat, cover and simmer until chicken is completely cooked, about 1 ½ hours. Remove chicken and place on a platter to cool. Skim fat off top of broth. After chicken is cooled, pull off skin and discard. Pull meat off bones and break into bite-size pieces. Return chicken pieces to broth. Add salt and pepper to taste. Place flour in a medium mixing bowl. Cut in the shortening until it resembles coarse crumbs. Add milk and mix until dough forms. Shape into a ball and cut in half. Place ½ the dough on a lightly floured surface and roll it out to about 1/8 inch. Cut into strips. Set aside. Repeat process with the remaining ½ dough. In the meantime, bring broth to a boil. Place dough strips (dumplings) into the broth and boil for about 20 minutes. Broth will thicken. Serve chicken and dumplings with your favorite vegetable.

Chicken Pot Pie

3 tbs. canola oil, divided
1 ½ lbs. boneless, skinless chicken breast, cut into 1 inch cubes
1 medium onion, chopped
2 garlic cloves, chopped
2 carrots, peeled and chopped
2 ribs celery, chopped
3 tbs. flour
1 cup sliced mushrooms
½ cup white wine
½ cup chicken broth
½ cup milk or half and half
Salt and pepper
1 sheet puff pastry
Flour

In a large skillet, heat 2 tbs. oil over low-medium heat. Cook chicken until cubes are cooked through. Drain. Set chicken aside. In same skillet, heat remaining 1 tbs. oil over low-medium heat. Sauté onion, garlic, carrots, and celery until onions become transparent. Whisk in flour and stir to make roux. Slowly stir in wine, chicken broth, and milk (or half and half). Stir in mushrooms and cooked chicken cubes. Add salt and pepper to taste. Pour mixture into a casserole dish or a baking dish. Place puff pastry sheet on lightly floured surface. Lightly sprinkle with flour and gently roll with rolling pin just to remove creases. Cover casserole or baking dish and crimp edges sealing completely. Vent pastry by making several slits. Bake at 350 degrees for 30–40 minutes or until pastry becomes golden brown.

Lemon Twisted Barbequed Chicken

1 whole chicken cut into 8 pieces
Salt and pepper
1 stick butter
Juice of 1 lemon
2 tbs. Worcestershire sauce
2 tbs. of your favorite barbeque sauce
1 clove garlic, minced

Place chicken pieces in a baking pan. Sprinkle with salt and pepper to taste. Place in the oven and bake at 350 degrees for 45 minutes. Meanwhile, in a medium saucepan, over low-medium heat, melt butter. Add lemon juice, Worcestershire sauce, barbeque sauce and garlic. Stir to blend. Coo for 10 minutes. Remove from heat and set aside. Once chicken has baked for 45 minutes, remove from oven and transfer to a tray. Baste chicken with butter mixture. Preheat grill on high. When ready, reduce heat to medium and place chicken on grill. Turn every 5 minutes, continually basting with remainder of sauce, for an additional 15–20 minutes.

PORK

Northern Recipes

John's Favorite Pot Roasted Pork Tenderloin

3tbs. canola oil
2 1½-lb. pork tenderloins both cut in half
2 medium onions, sliced into thick vertical slices
4 cloves garlic, chopped
1 large can sauerkraut
1 cup water
½ tsp. pepper
½ tsp. summer savory
½ tsp. caraway seeds

Heat 3 tbs. canola oil in large skillet over medium heat. Brown pork on all sides. Place onion slices and chopped garlic all around pork and cook until onions are browned. Add can of sauerkraut including liquid. Add water. Sprinkle with pepper, summer savory, and caraway seeds. Reduce heat and simmer for 1 hour. Remove pork from pan and slice into ½ inch slices. Serve over garlic smashed potatoes (see potato section for recipe) with sauerkraut, onion, garlic mixture and top with juice from pan.

Baked Pork Chops

4 pork loin chops, medium thickness
¾ cup mayonnaise
1 ½ cups Italian flavored breadcrumbs
Grated Romano or Parmesan cheese
Garlic powder
Onion powder
Salt and pepper

Brush pork chops with mayonnaise on both sides. Dip in breadcrumbs until well coated. Place in shallow roasting pan coated with non-stick spray. Sprinkle with garlic powder, onion powder, grated cheese, salt and pepper to taste. Bake at 350 degrees for 1 hour. Remove to platter. Serve with Old-Fashioned potato pancakes (see potato section for recipe) and applesauce.

Sweet and Sour Pork over Rice

2 tbs. canola oil
2 medium onions, sliced in thick chunks
½ cup water
1/3 cup white vinegar
¼ cup brown sugar
2 tbs. cornstarch
½ tsp. salt
¼ tsp. ground ginger
1 11-oz. can pineapple chunks, reserve liquid and add more pineapple juice to make 1 cup
1 ½ lbs. pork tenderloin cooked and sliced, cover to keep warm
1 medium green bell pepper, thinly sliced
1 medium red bell pepper, thinly sliced
1 15-oz. can sliced carrots, drained
White rice

In a large saucepan, heat oil over low-medium heat. Sauté onions until soft. In a small mixing bowl combine water, vinegar, sugar, cornstarch, salt, ginger, and pineapple juice. Pour over onions. Cook over low-medium heat until clear and thickened, whisking constantly to avoid lumps. Add meat, cover pan and cook for 30 minutes, stirring occasionally. Add pineapple chunks, peppers, and carrots. Cook 5 minutes longer until heated through. Meanwhile, cook white rice according to package directions. Serve immediately.

Glazed Roast Loin of Pork with Apples and Sweet Potatoes

1 4–5 lb. Pork loin roast (bone-in)
1 tsp. salt
1 tsp. garlic powder
½ tsp. ground black pepper
¾ cup orange marmalade
4 tsp. Worcestershire sauce
1 ½ cups apple juice
1 ½ tsp. lime juice
½ tsp. ground ginger
2 large Rome apples (about 1 pound)
2 large sweet potatoes cut into large round slices
2 tsp. cinnamon
2 tbs. flour
2 cups chicken broth

Rub pork roast with salt, garlic powder, and pepper. Place fat side up in shallow roasting pan. Insert meat thermometer into center of roast. Do not let it touch bones. Place pan in 325 degree oven for 2 ¼–2 ½ hours until thermometer reaches 170 degrees. In the meantime, in a small bowl, mix orange marmalade, Worcestershire sauce, apple juice, lime juice and ground ginger. After 1 hour of roasting, brush pork roast with marmalade mixture, and baste with remaining mixture every 20 minutes. After 1 ¾ hours of roasting, cut apples into thick wedges and add to pan surrounding roast along with sweet potato slices. Continue roasting. Stir apples and sweet potatoes occasionally.

When roast is done, remove from oven onto large platter. Let stand for 15 minutes before slicing. Place apple wedges and sweet potatoes in covered serving bowl, sprinkle with cinnamon.

Pour drippings into small sauté pan. Heat on low. Whisk in flour to make roux. Slowly add chicken broth, whisking constantly to avoid lumps forming. Continue to stir until gravy thickens. Remove from heat. Serve pork with gravy, apples and sweet potatoes.

Southern Recipes

Fried Pork Chops

1 cup milk
2 eggs
3 cups flour
1/3 cup seasoned salt
1 tsp. black pepper
1 tsp. baking powder
6–8 1-inch thick pork chops
Peanut oil

In a small bowl, beat eggs with milk. Set aside. In a medium mixing bowl, combine flour, seasoned salt, pepper, and baking powder until well blended. Pour into large Ziploc bag. Dip pork chops one at a time into egg mixture. Place pork chops on at a time into Ziploc bag and shake. In the meantime, heat 1-2 inches peanut oil in a large frying pan to about 350 degrees. Gently place pork chops into hot oil and fry approximately 6 minutes on each side. Drain on paper towels. Serve immediately.

Stuffed Pork Tenderloin

1 whole pork tenderloin (packaged in 2 pieces)
2 cups stuffing (recipe follows)
10–12 slices of center-cut bacon
¼ cup Balsamic vinegar
¼ cup low-salt chicken broth
1 clove garlic, minced
Salt and pepper

Butterfly each pork tenderloin. Place 1 tenderloin in a large roasting pan. Top with the stuffing. Place 2nd tenderloin on top of stuffing. Place bacon strips across top of pork roast until totally covered. In a small mixing bowl, blend together the vinegar, chicken broth, garlic and salt and pepper to taste. Pour mixture over pork. Place roasting pan in the oven and bake at 350 degrees for 1 ½ hours, until bacon is crisp and pork is cooked through.

For stuffing see Southern recipes in Casserole Section.

Barbequed Baby Back Ribs

2–3 full racks baby back ribs
Juice of 1 lemon (approximately 1/3 cup)
Seasoned salt
Pepper
1 bottle of your favorite barbeque sauce

Preheat oven to 300 degrees. Place ribs on a baking sheet and rub with lemon juice. Sprinkle with seasoned salt and pepper to taste. Cover ribs with aluminum foil and place in oven. Cook for approximately 2–2 ½ hours or until meat is nearly pulling away from rib bones. Heat grill on high. Brush ribs with barbeque sauce. Reduce heat to medium and place ribs on grill. Cook for 5 minutes on each side. Brush with barbeque sauce again and cook for 5 minutes on each side. Transfer to serving platter and serve hot.

Slow-Cooked Pork and Sauerkraut

3 tbs. olive oil
1 pork shoulder-blade roast
1 cup chicken broth
1 1-lb. bag of sauerkraut

Heat oil in a large skillet over medium heat. Brown pork shoulder blade on all sides. Remove. Place pork roast in a 6 quart crock pot. Pour chicken broth over roast. Cook on high heat approximately 3–4 hours or until bone in roast can be removed. Remove bone leaving roast in crock pot. Add sauerkraut with liquid. Continue to cook on high for 2 to 3 more hours or until sauerkraut has turned golden brown.

This has been a family favorite from my Grandmother Glass. We serve it with mashed potatoes and sliced tomatoes. Years ago this was cooked in the oven with water added every hour. I have made it much easier using a crock pot.

VEAL

Northern Recipes

Veal Osso Bucco

3 tbs. olive oil
4 veal shanks
1 medium onion, cut up
4 garlic cloves, chopped
2 carrots, pealed and cut up in small pieces
2 ribs of celery cut up in small pieces
½ lb. white mushrooms, sliced
1 14-oz. can beef broth
½ cup red wine
1 14-oz. can tomatoes, cut up, reserve liquid
½ tsp. summer savory
½ tsp. dried parsley
2 bay leaves

In a large pot, heat 3 tbs. olive oil over low–medium heat. Brown veal shanks on all sides. Remove from pot and transfer to plate. Set aside. In same pot, sauté onion, garlic, carrots, celery, and mushrooms until onions are slightly browned. Return veal shanks to pot. Add beef broth, wine, and tomatoes with reserved liquid. Sprinkle with summer savory and parsley. Add bay leaves. Bring to boil, reduce heat, cover and simmer for 2–2 ½ hours or until meat is almost falling off the bones. Remove bay leaves and discard. Serve veal in a soup bowl with vegetables and juices. Also great served over cooked orzo macaroni or plain couscous.

Veal Cutlets, Italian Style or French Style

Veal Marsala (Italian Style)

3 tbs. olive oil, divided
½ lb. fresh white mushrooms, sliced
1 ½ lbs. veal cutlets, cut very thin, flattened
Salt and pepper
Flour
½ cup Marsala wine

In a large sauté pan heat 1 tbs. olive oil over low-medium heat and cook mushrooms for 5 minutes. Remove mushrooms. Set aside. Sprinkle veal with salt and pepper to taste, flour lightly. In same pan, heat remaining olive oil over medium heat and sauté veal until browned on both sides. Add Marsala wine, cover, and simmer for 5 minutes. Add sautéed mushrooms and heat through.

Veal Francese (French Style)

1 ½ lbs. veal cutlets, cut very thin, flattened
1 cup flour
2 eggs, beaten with 2 tbs. milk
Salt and pepper
2 tbs. flour
½ cup dry white wine
1 cup low-salt chicken broth
2 tsp. lemon juice
3 tbs. olive oil

Flour veal; dip in egg mixture, flour veal again. Sprinkle with salt and pepper to taste. In a small bowl, stir together wine, broth, and lemon juice. Set aside. In sauté pan, heat olive oil over low-medium heat. Brown veal on both sides until cooked through. Remove from pan. Set aside. Whisk 2 tbs. flour into pan drippings to form a roux. Add wine, broth, and lemon juice mixture to pan stirring constantly. When mixture is smooth, return veal to pan and heat for 3–4 minutes, until some of the juice is absorbed into veal. Serve immediately pouring remaining juice over veal.

Veal Chops Paprika

1 cup flour
2 eggs
½ cup milk
2 cups plain bread crumbs
2 tbs. paprika, divided, plus 1 tsp.
1 tsp. cayenne pepper, divided
6 loin veal chops
3 tbs. canola oil
1 medium onion, chopped
3 garlic cloves, chopped
1 15-oz. can tomato sauce
1/3 cup water
Salt and pepper
1 tsp. dried parsley flakes
2 bay leaves
½ cup sour cream

Place flour in a shallow bowl. In a separate bowl, whisk together the eggs and milk. In a third bowl, blend together bread crumbs, 1 tbs. paprika, and ½ tsp. cayenne pepper. Dip each veal chop separately into flour, then egg mixture, and then cover completely with bread crumb mixture. In a large skillet, heat oil over medium heat. Brown veal chops on both sides. Drain. Transfer to a shallow baking dish. Sauté onion and garlic in same skillet until onions become soft. Add tomato sauce and water. Salt and pepper to taste. Sprinkle with remaining ½ tsp. cayenne pepper, and remaining tbs. paprika. Add parsley and bay leaves. Stir to blend. Remove from heat. Gently stir in sour cream. Pour over veal chops. Sprinkle with remaining tsp. paprika. Bake at 350 degrees for 50 minutes. Remove bay leaves and discard. Serve with your favorite side dishes.

Veal Parmigiana

2 cups Italian flavored breadcrumbs
¼ cup grated Romano cheese
1 ½ lbs. veal slices, cut very thin, flattened
1 cup flour
2 eggs, beaten with 2 tbs. milk
½ cup olive oil
1 quart basic tomato sauce (see Pasta section for recipe)
½ lb. mozzarella cheese, shredded

In small bowl, combine breadcrumbs with Romano cheese and toss lightly. Transfer ½ of the mixture to plate, reserve remaining mixture. Flour the veal; dip in egg mixture, then into breadcrumb mixture. Use reserved breadcrumb mixture if needed. In large skillet, heat ¼ cup olive oil over medium heat. Cook a few cutlets at a time in oil until browned on both sides. If more oil is needed, use remaining oil. Remove from pan and drain on paper towels. In a large baking dish, spoon tomato sauce until bottom of pan is covered. Place veal cutlets over sauce. Spoon a bit more sauce over cutlets, but do not cover them completely. Sprinkle with shredded mozzarella cheese. Bake at 350 degrees for 35–40 minutes or until sauce is bubbly. Serve with your favorite pasta as a side dish.

Southern Recipes

Slow-Cooked Veal Stew

½ cup all-purpose flour
1 tsp. seasoned salt
½ tsp. pepper
2 lbs. veal cut into 1 inch cubes
3 tbs. olive oil
4 medium potatoes, peeled and cut into 1 inch cubes
1 small onion, chopped
½ cup chopped carrots
½ cup chopped celery
8 oz. sliced fresh white mushrooms
1 15-oz. can low-salt beef broth
1 cup sour cream

In a Ziploc bag, combine flour, seasoned salt and pepper. Place veal cubes, a few at a time, into bag and shake well to coat. Heat oil in a large frying pan over low-medium heat. Add veal cubes and brown on all sides. Transfer veal to a platter lined with paper towels to soak up excess oil. Place veal cubes into crock pot. Add all remaining ingredients except sour cream. Set crock pot on low and cook for approximately 8 hours. Set on high for 1 hour. Blend in sour cream. Turn off crock pot. Serve over noodles or rice immediately.

Veal Chops with Mushroom Sauce

2 tbs. olive oil
4 veal chops, 1 inch thick
1 small onion, chopped
1 clove garlic, minced
¼ cup white wine
¼ cup chicken broth
Salt and pepper
1 8-oz. package sliced white mushrooms
½ cup sour cream

Heat oil in a large skillet over medium heat. Brown veal chops on both sides. Remove chops from skillet. Sauté onion and garlic in drippings. Stir in wine and broth. Salt and pepper to taste. Return veal chops to skillet, reduce heat and simmer about 10 minutes. Add mushrooms. Simmer an additional 10 minutes. Stir in sour cream. Remove from heat and serve immediately.

Lemon Grilled Veal Chops

4 1–1 ½ inch thick veal chops
¼ cup olive oil
Juice of ½ lemon, plus the squeezed ½ lemon
2 tbs. chopped fresh basil
2 tbs. Worcestershire sauce

Place chops in a Ziploc bag. In a small mixing bowl, combine olive oil, lemon juice, the squeezed ½ lemon, the basil and Worcestershire sauce. Pour mixture into the Ziploc bag, covering the veal chops. Marinate for at least 2 hours in the refrigerator. When ready, preheat grill on high. Reduce heat to low-medium. Place chops on grill. Cook for 10 minutes. Brush on a little of the marinade. Turn chops and cook for 10 minutes. Brush on a little more of the marinade. Repeat this process one more time on each side. Transfer chops to a serving platter. Great served over sautéed spinach and mushrooms or your favorite side dishes.

Veal Cutlets in Lemon-Butter Sauce

1 cup flour
½ cup flavored bread crumbs
1 tsp. garlic salt
½ tsp. pepper
1 egg
½ cup milk
1 ½ lbs. veal cutlets, thinly sliced
4 tbs. olive oil
4 tbs. butter
Juice of 1 lemon (approximately 1/3 cup)
1 ½ cups low-salt chicken broth

Place flour, bread crumbs, garlic salt and pepper in a Ziploc bag. Set aside. In a small bowl, stir together the egg and milk. Set aside. Place veal cutlets in egg wash one at a time and place into Ziploc bag. Shake until veal is completely covered with flour mixture. Meanwhile in a large skillet, heat oil over medium heat. Gently place a few cutlets at a time into oil and fry on both sides. Remove and drain on paper towels. Pour off all the oil and wipe pan with paper towels. Reduce heat to low and melt butter in same skillet. Add lemon juice and chicken broth. Simmer uncovered for about 10 minutes. Add veal cutlets and continue simmering for 5 minutes longer. Transfer veal cutlets to serving platter and spoon sauce over meat.

SEAFOOD

Northern Recipes

Shrimp Scampi over Angel Hair

1 ½ lbs. large shrimp, shelled and de-veined, leaving on tail section
¼ lb. butter (1 stick)
6 cloves garlic, chopped
2 tsp. parsley, finely chopped
2 tsp. flour
1/4 cup lemon juice
1 cup white wine
Salt and pepper
Grated Romano or Parmesan cheese

In sauté pan, heat butter until just melted. Add garlic and parsley and sauté until garlic is softened. Whisk in flour until smooth. Blend in lemon juice and wine, salt and pepper to taste. Add shrimp and sauté, constantly stirring until shrimp turn pink, about 5 minutes.

Meanwhile, cook ½–¾ lb. angel hair according to package directions. Drain. Serve shrimp and scampi sauce over angel hair. Sprinkle with cheese.

Baked Fish in Lemon, Wine, and Butter Sauce

1 ½ lbs. white fish (tilapia, flounder, grouper, cod, etc.)
¼ lb. butter (1 stick)
4 cloves garlic, minced
2 tsp. dried parsley
½ tsp. dried summer savory
½ tsp. dried marjoram
1 cup white wine
¼ cup lemon juice
Salt and pepper
½ cup flavored breadcrumbs
¼ cup grated Romano or Parmesan cheese

Place fish in a large baking dish. Melt butter over low heat. Remove from heat. Add garlic, parsley, summer savory, and marjoram. Blend in wine and lemon juice. Add salt and pepper to taste. Pour mixture over fish. Sprinkle fish with breadcrumbs and grated cheese. Bake at 350 degrees for 20–25 minutes, or until fish is flaky. Do not over bake.

Sautéed Scallops

1 lb. sea scallops
¾ cup flour
2 tbs. olive oil
1 tbs. butter
3 cloves garlic, minced
2 shallots, minced
2 tbs. lemon juice
2 tbs. sherry
1 tbs. spicy Dijon mustard
Salt and pepper
Lemon peel (optional)

Toss scallops lightly in flour. In a medium sauté pan heat oil over low-medium heat. Lightly brown the scallops in oil. Remove from pan with tongs to a platter. Heat butter in same pan. Sauté garlic and shallots. Add lemon juice, sherry and mustard. Whisk mixture until thickens slightly. Return scallops to pan, sprinkle with salt and pepper to taste. Heat through. Remove scallops to serving platter. Spoon sauce over scallops. Top with lemon peel if desired.

Poached Salmon

2 tbs. butter
1 carrot, peeled, cut into small bits
1 rib of celery, cut into small bits
1 small onion, finely chopped
2 garlic cloves, finely chopped
1 4-oz. can sliced mushrooms, drained
1 14 ½-oz. can low-salt chicken broth
½ cup white wine
6 salmon fillets
Salt and pepper
Fresh parsley, finely chopped

Melt butter in large skillet. Sauté carrot, celery, onion, garlic, and mushrooms until onion becomes transparent. Add broth and wine. Gently place salmon fillets in skillet. Add salt and pepper to taste. Bring liquid to a gentle boil, reduce heat, cover and simmer for about 10–15 minutes, or until salmon fillets are cooked through. Remove to serving platter, garnish with chopped parsley.

Southern Recipes

Crab Cakes

1 lb. jumbo lump crab meat
½ cup finely chopped onion
½ cup finely chopped red bell pepper, green bell pepper, and celery mixed together
¼ cup mayonnaise
2 tbs. yellow mustard
1 tsp. hot sauce
1 tsp Old Bay seasoning
1 egg
1 cup flavored bread crumbs
Vegetable oil or peanut oil

Pick through crab meat to clean out any shells. In a medium mixing bowl, combine crab first eight ingredients until well-blended. Mixture will seem loose. Form into cakes and pat them into bread crumbs on all sides. Pour about ¼ inch–½ inch oil into frying pan. Heat oil over low–medium heat to about 350 degrees. Gently place crab cakes into hot oil and fry on both sides until golden brown. Drain on paper towels. Serve immediately.

Low-Country Shrimp and Grits

3 tbs. olive oil, divided
½ lb. Cajun sausage, remove casings
1 small onion, chopped
1 clove garlic, minced
2 tbs. flour
1 small tomato, chopped
1 cup chicken broth
½ cup heavy whipping cream
3–5 dashes hot sauce
Salt and pepper
1 ½ lbs. shrimp, peeled and de-veined

In a large skillet, heat 2 tbs. oil over low-medium heat. Sauté sausage until browned. Drain to remove excess oil. Heat remaining 1 tbs. oil and sauté the onion and garlic. Stir in flour. Add chopped tomato, chicken broth, heavy cream, and hot sauce. Salt and pepper to taste. Stir until slightly thickened. Return sausage to skillet and simmer 10–15 minutes. Add shrimp and continue simmering until shrimp turn pink.

For grits recipe, see Southern Breakfast Section.

Beer-Battered Grouper

1 ½ cups all-purpose flour
4 tbs. seasoned salt
1 ¼ cups beer
5 dashes hot sauce
2 lbs. grouper, cut into 1 inch pieces

In a medium mixing bowl, whisk together the flour, seasoned salt, beer and hot sauce until mixture is smooth. Heat 2 cups oil in a large skillet (or heat oil in a deep fryer according to instructions). Drop grouper pieces in batter, a few at a time. Fry fish until golden brown, approximately 4–5 minutes. Fish will usually float to the top when it is close to completion. Place cooked pieces on a serving platter lined with paper towels to remove excess oil. Continue cooking remainder of fish in the same manner. Delicious served with a side of cole slaw and some sweet bread.

Bacon-Wrapped Shrimp

1 lb. large shrimp, peeled and de-veined, leave tails on
1 lb. center cut bacon
1 bottle of Cajun marinade
Juice of 1 orange

Wrap a slice of bacon around each shrimp. Using 3-4 inch wooden skewers that have been soaked in water, slide each bacon-wrapped shrimp individually onto end of skewer and push down about an inch. When all shrimp have been skewered, place them in a large Ziploc bag. Pour marinade and orange juice into bag and shake well. Close top of bag and refrigerate for 1–2 hours. Preheat outdoor grill on high. Reduce heat to medium. Place shrimp on grill and cook, turning occasionally, until shrimp turn pink and bacon is very crisp. Transfer to serving platter and serve immediately. Great served with rice and your favorite vegetable.

PASTA

Northern Recipes

Basic Tomato Sauce
(for Spaghetti and Meatballs or Your Favorite Pasta)

3 tbs. olive oil
1 large onion, chopped
6 cloves garlic, chopped
2 28-oz. cans tomato puree
1 28-oz. can whole tomatoes in puree, roughly chopped, reserve puree
1 15-oz. can tomato sauce
1 ½ cups water
½ cup red wine
½ cup fresh basil, roughly chopped (1 tsp. dried may be used)
¼ cup fresh oregano, roughly chopped (½ tsp. dried may be used)
½ cup fresh Italian parsley, roughly chopped (1 tsp. dried may be used)
¼ cup fresh marjoram, roughly chopped (½ tsp. dried may be used)
Salt and pepper
1 tsp. sugar

Heat oil in large pot. Sauté onion and garlic until onion becomes transparent. Do not brown. Add puree, tomatoes, tomato sauce, water, wine. Stir until blended. Add basil, oregano, parsley, marjoram, salt and pepper to taste, and sugar. Stir until well blended. Cook over low heat, stirring every 10–15 minutes, to prevent sauce from burning on bottom of pot. Let sauce simmer for about 3 hours, until sauce thickens a bit. After 1 hour of simmering, add meatballs (recipe below) and Italian sausages (hot or mild) that have already been browned on all sides. Serve over spaghetti or your favorite pasta cooked according to package directions.

Meatballs

1 ½ lbs. lean ground beef
½ lb. ground pork
2 eggs, lightly beaten
Salt and pepper
1/2 tsp. dried oregano
1 tsp. dried basil
1 tsp. dried parsley
½ tsp. dried marjoram
1 tsp. garlic powder
¼ tsp. onion powder
½ cup grated Romano or Parmesan cheese
1 cup Italian flavored breadcrumbs
¾ cup milk

In large bowl, using hands or wooden spoon, mix ground beef and pork until blended. Add eggs and salt and pepper to taste. Add next 7 ingredients. Mix well. In small bowl, combine breadcrumbs and milk until all milk is absorbed, leaving a slightly wet mixture. Add to meat mixture and blend well. Form meatballs. Either brown on all sides in a large frying pan, or place in baking dish and bake at 375 degrees for 45 minutes, or until browned on both sides, turning once half way through. Remove and add to tomato sauce after 1 hour of simmering. Makes about 22–24 meatballs.

Homemade Baked Manicotti and Cannelloni

Pancakes

3 eggs, at room temperature
1 cup flour
1 ½ cups milk
1 tbs. oil
Salt

Beat eggs. Gradually add flour, stirring constantly. Add milk, oil and salt. Stir to make a smooth batter. Do not over beat.

Heat a crepe pan or medium-sized non-stick pan thoroughly over medium heat. Coat with non-stick spray. Place 1/8–1/4 cup of batter in the middle of the pan, working rapidly roll the pan until batter covers the bottom. Cook the pancake until the sides start to curl and the bottom browns. Do not turn it over. With a spatula, carefully remove pancake from pan and transfer to a plate. You can stack the pancakes on top of each other on the plate because they will not stick to each other! After they are cooled, you may cover them with plastic wrap and refrigerate for several days or until ready to use.

Ricotta Filling (Manicotti)

1 2-lb. container whole milk or part-skim ricotta cheese
1 egg, lightly beaten
Dash salt
¼ cup fresh Italian parsley, finely chopped

1 cup, plus ½ cup shredded mozzarella cheese
¼ cup grated Romano or Parmesan cheese
1 package frozen spinach, cooked, cooled, and thoroughly drained
(optional)

Prepare filling the day you plan to use it. In a bowl, beat ricotta with
wooden spoon. Add egg and salt, blend well. Add parsley, 1 cup
mozzarella cheese, and grated cheese. If using spinach, it may be added
at this point and blended well. Spoon tomato sauce in the bottom of a
baking dish. Place pancakes one at a time on a flat surface. Place about
2 tablespoonfuls of ricotta filling in the middle of the pancake. Roll it
up, jellyroll style, and place seam side down in baking dish. Spoon
more tomato sauce over pancakes (do not totally cover). Sprinkle with
½ cup mozzarella cheese. Bake at 350 degrees for 30–40 minutes.

Meat Filling (Cannelloni)

1 lb. lean ground beef
½ lb. ground pork or veal
2 eggs, beaten
½ tsp. dried basil
¼ tsp. dried oregano
½ tsp. dried parsley
1/2 tsp. garlic powder
¼ tsp. onion powder
Salt and pepper
½ cup grated Romano or Parmesan cheese
¾ cup Italian flavored breadcrumbs
½ cup milk
½ cup shredded mozzarella cheese

In large bowl, using hands or wooden spoon, mix beef and veal until
blended. Add eggs. Mix well. Add basil, oregano, parsley, garlic
powder, onion powder, salt and pepper to taste. Blend in grated cheese.
In a small bowl, combine breadcrumbs with milk, until milk is

absorbed, leaving a wet mixture. Add breadcrumb mixture to meat mixture and blend well. Spoon tomato sauce in the bottom of a large baking dish. Place pancakes one at a time on a flat surface. Place about 2 tablespoonfuls of meat filling in the middle of the pancake. Roll up, jellyroll style, and place seam side down in baking dish. Spoon more tomato sauce over pancakes (do not totally cover.) Sprinkle with mozzarella cheese. Bake at 350 degrees for 30–40 minutes.

Penne a la Vodka

2 tbs. olive oil
1 medium onion, chopped
4 cloves garlic, chopped
1 28-oz. can tomato puree
1 28-oz. can tomatoes in puree, chopped, reserve liquid
1 8-oz. can tomato sauce
½ can water
¼ cup fresh basil, chopped (1/2 tsp. dried basil may be used)
1/8 cup fresh oregano, chopped (1/4 tsp. dried basil may be used)
¼ cup fresh Italian parsley, chopped (1/2 tsp. dried parsley may be used)
1/8 cup fresh marjoram, chopped (1/4 tsp. dried marjoram may be used)
Salt and pepper
1 cup vodka
1 cup half and half

In a sauce pan, heat olive oil over low heat. Sauté onion and garlic, until onion becomes transparent, do not brown. Add puree, tomatoes with liquid, tomato sauce, and water. Blend well. Add basil, oregano, parsley, marjoram, salt and pepper to taste. Stir until well blended. Simmer for 1 hour, stirring every 10 minutes to keep sauce from sticking to bottom of sauce pan. Add vodka. Simmer 1 hour more. Slowly stir in half and half until well blended. Heat through. In the meantime, cook penne pasta according to package directions, drain. Transfer to serving bowl. This sauce is great over penne pasta, but you can also use rigatoni, bowtie pasta, cheese or meat ravioli, or cheese or meat tortellini, or any pasta of your choice.

Italian Sausage and Peppers

2 lbs. mild Italian sausage
2 lbs. hot Italian sausage
3 tbs. olive oil
2 large onions cut into large pieces
6 cloves garlic, chopped
1 28-oz. can tomato sauce
1 12-oz. can tomato paste
¾ cup water
½ cup fresh basil, chopped (1 tsp. dried basil may be used)
¼ cup fresh oregano, chopped (1/2 tsp. dried oregano may be used)
½ cup fresh Italian parsley, chopped (1 tsp. dried parsley may be used)
¼ cup fresh marjoram, chopped (1/2 tsp. dried marjoram may be used)
Salt and pepper
1 large green bell pepper, deseeded and cut into strips
1 medium red bell pepper, deseeded and cut into strips
1 medium yellow bell pepper, deseeded and cut into strips
Bowtie pasta (or your favorite pasta)

Place sausage on a broiler pan tray, and bake at 375 degrees for 45 minutes to an hour, turning once halfway through bake time. Transfer to cutting board, and cut into angled slices about ½ inch thick. Set aside. In the meantime, in a large saucepan, heat olive oil over low-medium heat. Sauté onions and garlic, until onions are transparent, do not brown. Add tomato sauce, tomato paste and water. Blend well. Add basil, oregano, parsley, marjoram, salt and pepper to taste. Blend well. Add sausage slices and stir. Bring to a light boil and reduce heat. Simmer for 2 hours, stirring every 10 minutes to keep sauce from sticking to bottom of pan. Meanwhile, cook pasta according to package directions. Drain. Serve sausage and peppers over pasta. Sprinkle with grated Romano or Parmesan cheese. May also be served over rice or on Italian bread or hoagie roll as a hot sandwich with melted mozzarella cheese.

Southern Recipes

Cheesy Macaroni and Cheese

1 stick butter
2 cups milk
1 ¾ lbs. processed cheese block, cut up into chunks
2 cups shredded sharp cheddar cheese, divided
1 1-lb. box elbow macaroni or small shell macaroni
Salt and pepper

In a medium saucepan over low-medium heat, blend together butter, milk and processed cheese, stirring often. Add 1 1/2 cups shredded cheddar cheese. Lower heat to keep warm. In the meantime, cook macaroni according to package directions until al dente. Drain. In a large mixing bowl, combine macaroni and cheese mixture and stir until well blended. Grease a 2 ½ quart casserole dish or a 9 x 13 baking pan. Pour the macaroni mixture into prepared dish. Bake at 350 degrees for 45 minutes. Remove from oven. Sprinkle with remaining ½ cup shredded cheddar cheese. Return to oven and bake for an additional 15 minutes or until cheese on top is melted and lightly browned.

Use as a side dish or add chopped ham steak before baking and use as an entrée.

Shrimp and Spinach Scampi over Linguini

1 stick butter
2 tbs. olive oil
1 small shallot, finely chopped
2 cloves garlic, minced
1 tbs. flour
2 cups of washed fresh spinach leaves
Juice of 1 lemon (approximately 1/3 cup)
1 14 ½-oz. can low-salt chicken broth
1 cup white wine
1 lb. large shrimp, peeled and de-veined
1 1-lb. box linguini

In a large skillet, heat butter and oil over low-medium heat. Add shallots and sauté for about 5 minutes. Add garlic. Whisk in flour until lumps are gone. Add spinach leaves, lemon juice, chicken broth, and wine. Simmer until sauce reduces to about 1/3. Add shrimp and continue simmering until shrimp turn pink. Meanwhile cook linguini according to package directions. Drain. In a large pasta bowl, combine pasta with shrimp mixture and serve immediately.

Mom's Idea of Italian Pasta Southern Style

4 Italian sausages with meat squeezed from casings
1 large zucchini, split in half lengthwise, then sliced in ½ inch slices
½ sweet onion, chopped
1 clove garlic, finely chopped
8 oz. container sliced white mushrooms
1/3 cup red wine
1 14 ½-oz. can stewed tomatoes, chopped, reserve liquid
½ lb. rotini pasta
1 ¾ cups shredded mozzarella cheese

In a medium pot over low-medium heat, sauté sausage meat until all pink is gone. Drain. Return to pot. Add zucchini and onion. Sauté until tender. Add garlic and mushrooms and continue cooking for 4–5 minutes. Add red wine and stewed tomatoes. Simmer for 10 minutes. Meanwhile, cook pasta according to package directions. Drain. Stir pasta into sauce and pour into greased 2 quart casserole dish. Top with mozzarella cheese. Bake at 350 degrees for 40 minutes or until cheese is lightly browned and sauce is bubbly.

Honey Mustard Chicken Pasta

1 lb. boneless chicken breast
1 lb. rotini pasta
3 large green onions, finely chopped
1 small red pepper, finely chopped

Sauce

1/3 cup honey mustard
1 ½ cups mayonnaise
1 tbs. dried parsley flakes
Salt and pepper

Poach chicken breasts in skillet filled with ½ inch water. Remove from skillet and cut into ½ inch chunks. Meanwhile, cook pasta according to package directions. Drain. Toss pasta with chicken, onions, and red pepper. Let cool for 30 minutes. Stir in honey mustard, mayonnaise, and parsley. Mix well. Salt and pepper to taste. Chill for 1–2 hours before serving.

VEGETABLES

Northern Recipes

Broccoli, Cauliflower and Baby Carrots Almandine

2 lbs. fresh broccoli
1 small head of cauliflower
1 bag baby carrots
2 tbs. olive oil
1 medium onion, thinly sliced
2 cloves garlic, crushed
1 4 oz. bag sliced almonds
¼ cup real bacon bits

Cut thick lower stems off broccoli and cut off any leaves, wash well, drain. Cut cauliflower florets off stem, wash well, drain. Place in a vegetable steamer with baby carrots. Steam until broccoli turns bright green and cauliflower and carrots are soft, but not mushy. Transfer to a serving bowl. Meanwhile, while vegetables are steaming, heat olive oil in a small skillet. Sauté onions, garlic and almonds, until onions begin to brown lightly. Remove from heat. Add onion, garlic and almond mixture to beans. Add bacon bits. Toss until combined. Serve immediately.

Steamed Spaghetti Squash Italiano

1 medium sized spaghetti squash
3 tbs. olive oil
1 medium onion, chopped
4 cloves garlic, chopped
1 15-oz. can Italian Style Stewed Tomatoes
Salt and pepper
1 15-oz. jar whole mushrooms, drained
1 15-oz. can quartered artichoke hearts, drained
1 15-oz. can small ripe pitted black olives, drained
Grated Romano or Parmesan cheese

Cut squash in half lengthwise. Remove seeds. Place rind-side up in a shallow pan. Pour about ½ inch water around squash. Bring to boil, cover and simmer for about 30 minutes, or until squash is softened, but not mushy. Remove from pan, let cool for a while. Meanwhile, heat olive oil in a medium saucepan over low-medium heat. Sauté onion and garlic, just until onion becomes transparent (do not brown). Pour in tomatoes. Add salt and pepper to taste. Add mushrooms, artichoke hearts, and olives. Simmer over low heat for about 20–30 minutes. While sauce is simmering, using a fork, scrape the squash out of the rind and transfer to bowl. It will resemble strands of spaghetti. When sauce is finished simmering, pour over squash and toss until just combined. Sprinkle with grated cheese. Can be used as a side dish or an entrée.

Creamed Spinach and Potatoes

3 medium potatoes, peeled and diced
2 tbs. butter
1 cup onions, finely chopped
3 cloves garlic, minced
3 tbs. flour
1 ½ cups milk
Salt and pepper
2 packages baby spinach leaves

Place diced potatoes in the top of a double boiler. Over medium heat, steam potatoes until just softened. Do not over cook. Drain. Set aside in a serving bowl. Meanwhile, in a small pan, heat butter over low-medium heat. Sauté onions and minced garlic for 2–3 minutes. Whisk in flour to make a roux. Slowly add milk stirring constantly until sauce thickens. Add salt and pepper to taste. Keep warm over low heat. In a large skillet or sauce pan, bring about a cup of water to a boil, and add spinach leaves a little at a time, turning quickly with tongs. As leaves begin to wilt, quickly remove to strainer to drain. Combine spinach with potatoes in the serving bowl. Pour cream sauce over spinach. Serve immediately.

Carrot Soufflé

2 cups carrots (1 1-lb bag), peeled and cut into ½ inch pieces
½ cup butter or margarine (1 stick)
1 tsp. baking powder
½ tsp. cinnamon
½ cup sugar
5 tbs. flour
3 eggs, separated
Cinnamon for topping

Cook carrots in water until very soft. Drain. Place in large mixing bowl. Using hand masher, mash carrots with butter. Add baking powder, cinnamon, sugar, and flour. Mix well using electric mixer. Add egg yolks and blend well. In a separate bowl, with clean beaters, beat egg whites stiff, but not dry. Gently fold into carrot mixture until just combined. Pour into greased 1 ½–2 quart casserole. Sprinkle top with more cinnamon. Bake at 400 degrees for 15 minutes. Reduce heat to 350 degrees and continue baking for 45 minutes until top is browned. Serve hot.

Southern Recipes

Tasty Collard Greens

4 cups water
2 cups chicken broth
1 ham steak cut into cubes
1 bag chopped pre-washed collard greens
1 tsp red pepper flakes
½ tsp. salt
¼ tsp. black pepper

Pour water and broth in a 3 quart soup pot. Add cubed ham. Boil, uncovered, until liquid is reduced to one half. Add collard greens and seasonings. Cook, covered, for approximately 30 minutes or until very tender. Transfer to serving bowl and serve immediately.

Aunt Marilyn's Baked Squash

1 ½–2 lbs. yellow squash, cut into bite-size pieces
1 small onion, finely chopped
3 eggs
¾ cup mayonnaise
1 cup grated Parmesan cheese
1 tsp. salt
2 slices of toast, crumbled

Place squash in a medium saucepan and cover with water. Boil until tender. Drain. Transfer to a medium mixing bowl. Add onion to squash. In a separate medium mixing bowl combine eggs, mayonnaise, Parmesan cheese, and salt. Add squash and onion mixture. Mash lightly with potato masher. Lightly grease a 9 x 11 baking pan. Pour in the squash mixture. Top with crumbled toast. Bake at 350 degrees for approximately 45 minutes or until a toothpick inserted in center comes out clean. Serve immediately.

Baked Onions and Mushrooms

4 large sweet Vidalia onions
¼ cup red wine
4 beef bouillon cubes
5 tbs. butter
8 oz. baby Bella mushrooms, sliced

Cut onions into quarters and place into a casserole dish. Add wine and beef bouillon cubes. Dot with butter. Cover and bake at 375 degrees for 45 minutes. Remove from oven and add mushrooms. Cover and return to oven for 20–25 minutes more. Serve hot.

Sautéed Cabbage and Bacon

1 head cabbage, chopped
4–5 slices bacon, cooked until crisp and drained
3 tbs. butter
Salt and pepper

Place cabbage in a large pot and cover with water. Over high heat, bring cabbage to a boil and cook for approximately 5 minutes. (If you like crispier cabbage, then omit this step.) Drain cabbage well. Break up cooked bacon into bits. In a large skillet, melt butter over low- medium heat. Add cabbage, salt and pepper to taste. Sauté cabbage for about 10 minutes. Stir in bacon bits. Serve immediately.

POTATOES

Northern Recipes

Old-Fashioned Potato Pancakes
with Homemade Applesauce

6 medium potatoes, peeled and cut into large pieces
1 medium onion, quartered
2 eggs
¾ cup flour
1 tsp. baking powder
Salt and pepper
½ tsp. garlic powder
1 tsp. dried parsley
½ tsp. dried summer savory
3 cups peanut oil

Put 1 egg in blender. Add potatoes a few pieces at a time, blend on medium–high speed. Add onion quarters one at a time and blend until well combined. Pour potato mixture into strainer to remove much of the liquid. Pour into large mixing bowl. Using wooden spoon, stir in flour and baking powder, salt and pepper to taste, garlic powder, parsley and summer savory. Gently beat remaining egg in small bowl and stir into potato mixture. Mixture should resemble a thickened batter. Add a bit more flour if batter is too wet. In a large frying pan, heat 2 cups peanut oil over medium heat. When well heated reduce heat to low-medium. Tilt pan being careful not to spill oil, and using a large spoon, place a heaping spoonful of potato batter into dry part of pan. Slowly flatten pan letting oil surround potato batter. (If you place batter directly into hot oil, it will splatter and pancakes will not form correctly.) You should cook only 3 pancakes at a time to keep oil from cooling too much. Add additional oil to pan between batches, if needed. Let fresh oil get hot enough before cooking next batch of pancakes. When pancakes are browned on one side carefully turn them over and cook on other side until brown and crispy. Remove from pan onto paper towels to drain. Transfer to serving platter. Serve immediately with applesauce or sour cream.

Homemade Applesauce

2 large Granny Smith apples
2 large Fuji apples
2 large Golden Delicious apples
2 large Jonathan apples
1 ½ cups water
¼ cup sugar
1 tsp. cinnamon
1 tsp. allspice
½ tsp. nutmeg

Cut apples into quarters and remove cores. Leave skins on to add more flavor to applesauce. Place quartered apples in large pot and add water. (Apples do not have to be totally covered with water.) Bring to a boil, reduce heat, simmer, covered for 30–40 minutes or until apples are very soft. Drain. Squeeze apples through a sieve (leaving skins behind) into a large mixing bowl. Add sugar, cinnamon, allspice, and nutmeg. Stir until well blended. Refrigerate for several hours or overnight before serving.

Garlic Smashed Potatoes and Fluffy Mashed Potatoes

Garlic Smashed

6 large red skinned or white potatoes, peels left on and quartered
6 cloves garlic
¼ cup butter or margarine (½ stick)
¼ cup milk
Salt and pepper
2 tsp. dried parsley
½ tsp. summer savory

Place potatoes and garlic cloves in a large pot and completely cover with water. Bring to a boil and cook potatoes until soft, but not mushy (about 20 minutes.) Drain. Place potatoes and garlic in a large mixing bowl. Add butter, milk, salt and pepper to taste, parsley, and summer savory. Using hand masher, mash potatoes just until all ingredients are incorporated. Mixture should be lumpy. Serve with your favorite entrée.

Fluffy Mashed

4 large red skinned or white potatoes, peeled and quartered
3 cloves garlic
¼ cup butter or margarine (1/2 stick)
1 3-oz. package cream cheese, softened
1/3 cup half and half
Salt and pepper
1 tsp. dried parsley

Place potatoes and garlic cloves in a large pot. Cover completely with water. Bring to boil and cook potatoes until soft, but not mushy (about 20 minutes.) Drain. Place potatoes in a large mixing bowl. Add butter, cream cheese, half and half, salt and pepper to taste, and parsley. Using electric mixer, beat potatoes until very smooth and fluffy. Serve with your favorite entrée.

Hashed Brown Potatoes and Home Fries

Hashed Browns

3 medium potatoes, peeled and grated
1 small onion, peeled and grated
Salt and pepper
3 tbs. canola oil

Place grated potatoes in a mixing bowl. Cover potatoes completely with water and let soak for about 10 minutes. Drain. Repeat soaking process and drain well. Toss with grated onion. Meanwhile, heat canola oil in a large frying pan. Gently place potatoes and grated onion in oil trying not to splatter oil. Spread potatoes to cover entire bottom of pan. Salt and pepper to taste. Continue frying potatoes until browned. Turn over and let brown on other side until crispy. Serve immediately.

Home Fries

3 medium potatoes, peels left on and cut into large cubes
1 medium onion, sliced
1 small green bell pepper, cut into small pieces
2 tsp. seasoned salt
½ tsp. garlic powder
½ tsp. dried parsley

Heat 3 tbs. canola oil in a large frying pan. Gently place potatoes, onion, and green pepper in oil trying not to splatter oil. Sprinkle with seasoned salt, garlic powder, and parsley. Fry until potatoes are browned on all sides, turning frequently to avoid potatoes from sticking to pan.

Creamy Scalloped Potatoes

6 red skinned potatoes
¼ cup butter or margarine (½ stick)
¼ cup flour
2 cups milk
Salt and pepper
1 tsp. dried parsley flakes
2 cups shredded baby Swiss cheese

Wash and peel potatoes. Cut into ¼ inch slices. Place in a bowl and fill with water to keep potatoes from turning brown. Set aside. In a medium skillet, melt butter over low–medium heat. Whisk in flour to make a roux. Slowly pour in milk whisking constantly to keep sauce smooth. When sauce thickens, add salt and pepper to taste and parsley. Coat a 9 x 13 inch baking dish with non-stick spray. Place a layer of potatoes on bottom of dish. Spoon 1/3 of the sauce over potatoes. Sprinkle with 1/3 of the shredded cheese. Repeat 2 more times leaving off the last layer of the shredded cheese. Bake in a 425 degree oven for 1 hour or until potatoes are soft. Sprinkle last third of shredded Swiss cheese on top. Return to oven and continue baking for 20 minutes more or until cheese has melted on top.

Southern Recipes

A Touch of Sweetness Mashed Potatoes

4 large baking potatoes, peeled and cut into large chunks
1 large sweet potato, peeled and cut into large chunks
1 stick butter
1 8-oz. package cream cheese
½ cup half and half
½ cup Parmesan cheese
Salt and pepper

Place potatoes in a large pot and cover with water. Bring to a boil and cook for 15–18 minutes or until potatoes are tender. Drain. Transfer potatoes into a large mixing bowl. Add butter and cream cheese. Mash by hand with a potato masher. Add half and half, Parmesan cheese, and salt and pepper to taste. Using an electric mixer beat on medium speed for about 2 minutes. Transfer to serving dish or casserole dish. Serve immediately. Potatoes can also be made a day ahead of time, then baked, covered, at 350 degrees until heated through.

Ranch-Style Smashed Potatoes

3 lbs. Yukon Gold potatoes, cut into large chunks with skins on
1 ½ sticks butter
1 8-oz. sour cream
½ cup half and half
3 stalks green onion, diced
1 package dry ranch dressing mix
6 slices bacon, cooked crisp and crumbled
1 cup shredded cheddar cheese
Salt and pepper to taste

In a large pot add potatoes and cover with water. Bring to a boil and cook for 15–18 minutes or until tender. Drain. Transfer to a large mixing bowl. Add remaining ingredients. Mash by hand with a potato masher, leaving mixture lumpy. Serve immediately.

Cheesy "Hashed" Potatoes

1 bag of uncooked Shredded Hash Browns
1 cup cottage cheese (regular or low fat)
1 10 ¾-oz. can cream of mushroom soup
2 cups of shredded sharp cheddar cheese
¼ cup milk
¼ cup chopped green onions

In a large mixing bowl, combine all ingredients, reserving ½ cup of the cheddar cheese. Coat a 9 x 9 inch baking pan with non-stick cooking spray. Pour potato mixture into prepared pan. Top with remaining cheese. Cover and bake at 400 degrees for 45 minutes. Remove cover and bake an additional 15 minutes, or until browned on top.

Fried Potato Chips

2 large Idaho potatoes cut into very thin slices, leaving peels on
Peanut oil
Salt and pepper

In a deep fryer, heat oil to 375 degrees. Gently place potato slices into hot oil a few at a time and fry until crisp and golden brown. Remove with strainer onto paper towels. Salt and pepper to taste. Enjoy as a snack or as a side dish with your favorite sandwich or hamburger.

CASSEROLES

Northern Recipes

Cheesy Tuna Casserole

½ cup butter or margarine (1 stick)
½ cup flour
4 cups milk
¼ tsp. black pepper
1 ½ cups shredded sharp cheddar cheese
1 6-oz. can white albacore tuna packed in water, drained, set aside
1 package frozen peas, cooked according to package directions, drained
1 lb. pasta shells, cooked according to package directions, drained, set aside
Grated Romano or Parmesan cheese
½ cup bread crumbs for topping

Melt butter in a large sauté pan over low to medium heat. Remove from heat. Quickly whisk in flour, making a smooth roux. Return pan to heat and slowly add milk to roux, stirring constantly with whisk until sauce thickens. Add pepper. Gently stir in 1 cup shredded cheddar cheese until cheese is melted and well blended. Stir in tuna and peas. Add pasta to cheese mixture and stir until pasta is well coated. Coat a large casserole dish or large baking pan with non-stick spray. Gently pour pasta and cheese mixture into dish using scraper. Sprinkle with grated cheese and remaining ½ cup shredded cheddar cheese and top with bread crumbs. Bake at 350 degrees for 45 minutes, until breadcrumbs are golden brown.

Stewed Tomatoes, Squash, Zucchini, and Mushroom Casserole

1 medium onion, chopped
4 cloves garlic, chopped
2 14 ½ oz. cans Italian style stewed tomatoes
½ tsp. black pepper
2 cups yellow squash, cut into thin circles
2 cups zucchini, cut into thin circles
2 cups white mushroom slices
Grated Romano or Parmesan cheese
¼ lb. shredded mozzarella cheese

Heat 3 tbs. olive oil in a skillet over low heat. Sauté onion and garlic until onion is soft and transparent. Add stewed tomatoes and pepper. Simmer for 20 minutes. Remove from heat. Coat a large casserole dish with non-stick spray. Add squash, zucchini, and mushroom slices to stewed tomato mixture. Gently pour into prepared casserole dish. Sprinkle with grated Romano or Parmesan cheese and top with grated mozzarella cheese. Bake at 350 degrees for 45 minutes, until tomato mixture is bubbly and cheese is lightly browned on top.

Broccoli and Cheddar Quiche (or Quiche of Your Choice)

1 pie crust in 10 inch pie pan
1 package fresh broccoli florets
4 eggs
2 cups half and half
2 cups shredded sharp cheddar cheese

Place broccoli florets in top of a double boiler. Steam broccoli for about 4 minutes; do not over cook. Rinse in cold water and drain. In a large mixing bowl, beat eggs. Stir in half and half. Stir in cheddar cheese and blend well. Arrange broccoli florets in circle pattern on bottom of pie crust. Pour egg/cheese mixture over broccoli. Bake at 375 degrees for 45 minutes or until cake tester comes out clean and quiche is browned on top.

Variations

Spinach Mushroom Quiche
Use 1 package frozen spinach and 1 4 oz. jar mushroom slices instead of broccoli.
Use 2 cups shredded Monterey Jack cheese instead of cheddar cheese.
Eggs and half and half remain the same.

Quiche Lorraine

Use ½ lb. crisp bacon, crumbled, instead of vegetables.
Use 2 cups shredded Lorraine Swiss cheese instead of other cheeses.
Eggs and half and half remain the same.

Seafood Quiche

Use 1 cup small boiled shrimp and 1 cup crab meat, instead of vegetables.
Use 2 cups shredded mild white cheddar or Monterey Jack instead of other cheeses.
Eggs and half and half remain the same.

Ham and Cheese Quiche

Use 2 cups cooked ham, cut up in cubes, instead of vegetables.
Use 2 cups shredded American or Baby Swiss cheese instead of other cheeses.
Eggs and half and half remain the same.

Mexican Quiche

Use 2 cups browned ground beef, mixed with taco seasoning packet according to packet directions, instead of vegetables.
Use 2 cups shredded Colby cheese instead of other cheeses.
Eggs and half and half remain the same.

Shepherd's Pie (Meat and Potato Casserole)

¼ cup butter (1/2 stick)
¼ cup flour
½ tsp. pepper
1 cup milk
1 cup low-salt beef broth
4 cups cooked ground beef
½ cup cooked peas
½ cup cooked green beans
½ cup cooked corn
½ cup cooked carrots, diced
1 4-oz. can sliced mushrooms
1 jar pearl onions, drained
1 recipe for Fluffy Mashed Potatoes (found in Northern potato section)
Grated Parmesan cheese
1 tsp. dried parsley flakes
2 tbs. butter

In a large skillet, melt butter over low heat. Whisk in the flour and pepper to make a roux. Slowly pour in the milk and the broth, constantly stirring to keep lumps from forming. Once sauce is thickened, add ground beef, peas, green beans, mushrooms, corn, mushrooms, carrots, and pearl onions. Stir to blend. Spoon half the mashed potato mixture into the bottom of a greased 2 quart casserole. Cover with meat mixture. Spread remaining mashed potatoes evenly over top of meat mixture. Sprinkle with grated cheese and parsley flakes. Dot with butter. Bake at 375 for 30 minutes or until top is golden brown.

Southern Recipes

Chicken Divan Casserole

1 ½ lbs. boneless chicken breast, cut up in bite-size pieces
2 cups fresh or frozen broccoli florets
1 10 ¾-oz. can Cream of Chicken Soup
¾ cup mayonnaise
1 tbs. lemon juice
Salt and pepper
1 cup shredded cheddar cheese, divided
2 slices toast, crumbled

Place chicken pieces in the bottom of a 2 quart casserole dish. Add broccoli florets over chicken. In a small mixing bowl, combine soup, mayonnaise, lemon juice and ¾ cup of cheddar cheese, and salt and pepper to taste. Stir until well blended. Pour over chicken and broccoli. Sprinkle with crumbled toast and remaining ¼ cup cheddar cheese. Bake at 350 degrees, covered, for 45 minutes.

Sausage Stuffing

1 lb. Chorizo or Andouille sausage, remove casings
1 stick butter
1 small onion finely diced
4 ribs celery finely diced
2 cups chicken broth, plus 1 cup water
½ tsp. sage
Salt and pepper
1 loaf herbed bread, cut into cubes and dried overnight
1 lb. cornbread, crumbled and dried overnight

In a large saucepan, sauté sausage meat over medium heat. Drain. Set aside. In same pan, melt butter over medium heat. Add onion and celery and lightly sauté. Add chicken broth and water, sage, salt and pepper to taste. Stir to blend. Mix in dried bread cubes and drive cornbread crumbs until all liquid is absorbed. If using as a side dish, then at this point pour into a greased casserole dish. Bake at 375 degrees for 45 minutes, or until golden brown on top.

Chicken and Mushroom Noodle Casserole

1 8-oz. bag extra wide egg noodles
1 9.75-oz. can white chicken breast, drained
1 10 ¾-oz. can chicken and mushroom soup
1 cup mayonnaise
1 8-oz. package sliced white mushrooms
1 cup milk
1 ½ cups shredded cheddar cheese
1 cup crushed potato chips or crushed Ritz crackers

Cook noodles according to package directions. Drain. Pour noodles into greased 3 quart casserole dish. Add remaining ingredients, except potato chips (or crackers.) Mix together well. Sprinkle top with crushed potato chips or crackers. Bake at 350 degrees for approximately 40–50 minutes or until bubbly and crisp on top.

French Onion Chicken Casserole

4 chicken breasts
1 10 ¾-oz. can condensed French onion soup
1 8-oz. package white mushrooms, each cut in half
1 small can French fried onions
1 ½ cups shredded Swiss cheese

Place chicken breasts in a large casserole dish. Add soup and mushrooms. Bake at 350 degrees for 30 minutes. Remove from oven and top with French fried onions. Return to oven and bake for 15 minutes more. Remove from oven and top with Swiss cheese. Return to oven and continue baking until cheese has melted and becomes bubbly. This is great served over mashed potatoes.

DESSERTS

Northern Recipes

Old-Fashioned Apple Pie

Crust

2 ½ cups flour
1 tbs. sugar
Pinch of salt
Ice water
½ cup cold butter (1stick), cut into slivers
1/3 cup solid white vegetable shortening

Filling

8 medium Granny Smith apples, peeled, cored, sliced
2 tbs. lemon juice
¼ cup sugar
5 tbs. flour
1 tsp. ground cinnamon
½ tsp. ground nutmeg
½ tsp. ground allspice
2 tbs. butter
3 tbs. milk

In a large bowl, combine flour, sugar and salt, and toss lightly with a
fork. Add butter and shortening to flour and cut in with a pastry blender.
Mixture should be like coarse crumbs. Sprinkle with 5 tbs. ice water

and stir with a fork. If mixture is dry, add more water a tbs. at a time (do not make too wet.) Gather dough into a ball and wrap tightly with plastic wrap. Refrigerate at least 30 minutes. Remove dough from plastic wrap. Divide into two equal portions. Lightly flour a flat surface and roll out one portion of dough into a 12 inch circle. Always roll from center out to edges. Transfer dough to a 9 inch pie pan and trim overhang to about ½ inch over edge. Roll out remaining dough into another 12 inch circle. Set aside.

In a large bowl, toss sliced apples with lemon juice to keep them from turning brown. In a smaller bowl, combine sugar, flour, cinnamon, nutmeg and allspice. Sprinkle sugar mixture over apples and toss to coat evenly. In prepared pie pan, layer the apple slices in circles and keep mounding them so they are higher in the center. Dot the apples with butter. Place reserved crust over apples and trim to ½ inch overhang. Turn both edges of dough under and flute with fingers or press with fork tines. Vent top crust by making several slits. Brush dough with milk (do not soak.) Bake at 425 degrees for 15 minutes, reduce heat to 350 degrees and bake for 40 more minutes, or until crust is golden. Cool on a cake rack.

Mom's Creamy Rice Pudding

½ gallon 2% milk
1 cup white rice, uncooked
1 cup granulated sugar
1 tsp. vanilla
1 egg + 1 yolk, well beaten
1 egg white
Cinnamon and nutmeg to taste

Pour milk, rice and sugar in a large pot. Simmer over low-medium heat for approximately 1 ½ to 2 hours, stirring every 5–10 minutes to avoid skin from forming on top and sticking to bottom of pan. When mixture begins to lightly bubble, stir constantly for about 5 minutes. Remove from heat. Pour some hot rice mixture into beaten eggs, beating quickly to keep eggs from cooking. Pour back into rice mixture and stir until well combined. Stir in vanilla. In a small mixing bowl, beat egg white dry, but not stiff, or until peaks form on top. Gently fold meringue into rice mixture. Let stand to cool. Transfer to a large serving bowl. Sprinkle with cinnamon and nutmeg to taste. Refrigerate several hours before serving.

Grandma's Peach (or Apple) Tart

Crust

1 cup flour
2 tbs. sugar
½ cup butter or margarine (1 stick), cut into slivers
1 tbs. white vinegar

Filling

2 lbs. peaches (or apples), peeled, sliced
2 tbs. lemon juice
2 tbs. sugar
2 tbs. flour
1 tsp. cinnamon

Combine flour, sugar, and butter in a mixing bowl. Mix with fork until mixture resembles coarse crumbs. Sprinkle with vinegar and make into a ball and press into a 9 inch tart pan with removable bottom. In a separate bowl, toss peaches (or apples) with lemon juice, sugar, flour, and cinnamon. In prepared tart pan, layer the peaches (or apples) into circles. Do not mound higher in center. Bake at 350 degrees for 1 hour and 15 minutes or until edge of crust browns. Cool 30 min. before removing outer circle of tart pan. Great served warm with vanilla ice cream or whipped cream.

New York-Style Cheesecake

1 graham cracker crumb crust (recipe following) for 10-inch springform pan
2 ½ lbs. cream cheese (4 ½ 8-oz. bricks), softened
¾ cup sugar
3 eggs, lightly beaten
1 ½ tsp. vanilla
3 tbs. cornstarch
1 ½ cups sour cream

Preheat oven to 400 degrees. In a large mixing bowl, beat the cream cheese and sugar until smooth. Beat in eggs and vanilla. Stir in the cornstarch and sour cream until well blended. Pour cheese mixture into the prepared graham cracker crust. Bake for 45 minutes. Turn off oven. Prop the door slightly open. Let the cake cool in the oven for 2 hours. Chill several hours before serving.

Graham Cracker Crumb Crust

2 cups graham cracker crumbs
1 stick butter, melted
½ cup superfine sugar

In a medium mixing bowl, combine all ingredients until well blended. Using your fingers, press crumbs onto bottom and halfway up the sides of a 10-inch springform pan, making sure there is an even thickness of crumbs. Place in the refrigerator and let chill for at least 30 minutes before filling.

Southern Recipes

Mary-Lynn's Peanut Butter Pie

½ cup sugar
6 oz. cream cheese, softened
1 cup peanut butter
½ cup milk
8 oz. Cool Whip
1 ready-made graham cracker crust

In a medium mixing bowl, cream the sugar and cream cheese. Add peanut butter and stir until well blended. Fold in Cool Whip. Pour mixture into graham cracker crust. Freeze for at least 2 hours before serving. Serve with fresh blueberries or strawberries.

Glazed Rum Cake

Cake

1 package yellow cake mix
1 3.4-oz. vanilla pudding mix
4 eggs
½ cup water
½ cup vegetable oil
½ cup dark rum

Preheat oven to 325 degrees. Grease and flour a non-stick bundt pan. In a large mixing bowl, combine all ingredients. Using an electric mixer beat on low for 1 minute. On medium speed, beat an additional 2 minutes or until all ingredients are well blended. Pour mixture into prepared bundt pan. Bake for 1 hour. Remove from oven. Immediately poke holes into cake. Do not remove from pan.

Glaze

½ cup butter
¼ cup water
1 cup sugar
½ cup dark rum

In a medium saucepan combine all ingredients. Bring to a boil. Reduce heat and simmer, stirring constantly, until mixture thickens, about 8–10 minutes. While cake is still hot, pour glaze over cake. Glaze will soak into cake. Let cake cool for 10–15 minutes. Turn cake upside-down onto serving plate. Remove pan. Let cake cool completely before serving.

Savannah's Favorite Apple Crisp

4–5 large Granny Smith apples, peeled, cored and sliced
2 tsp. lemon juice
½ cup granulated sugar
2 tbs. all-purpose flour
1 ½ sticks butter, melted
1 cup dark brown sugar
2 cups old-fashioned oats
1 cup all-purpose flour

Grease a 9 x 9 inch baking pan. In a medium mixing bowl, combine apple slices, lemon juice, granulated sugar, and 2 tbs. flour. Place in prepared baking pan. In a separate medium mixing bowl, combine melted butter, dark brown sugar, oats and 1 cup flour. Mix well. Spoon oat mixture topping over the apples. Bake at 350 degrees for 45 minutes or until apples are tender and juice is bubbling and topping is golden brown. Serve warm with vanilla ice cream or whipped cream.

S'mores Pie

1 9-oz. graham cracker ready crust
1 5.9-oz package instant chocolate pudding
1 10-oz. bag of miniature marshmallows

Remove plastic cover from crust package. In a medium bowl, prepare chocolate pudding according to package directions. Pour pudding into crust. Refrigerate for approximately 30 minutes. Pour marshmallows on top of pudding. Set oven to broil. Place pie in oven and broil until marshmallows melt and brown a bit on top, taking care not to burn the marshmallows. Let cool just a bit before serving.

Printed in the United States
64754LVS00005B/169-270

9 781424 147991